10 KEYS
to
MAXIMIZING
Your
HEAVENLY
FICO SCORES

UNLOCKING THE SECRETS TO
HEAVENLY WEALTH AND PROSPERITY

DONNIE RAY FEATHERSTONE, SR.

CHRISTIAN LIVING
B O O K S
Largo, MD

Christian Living Books, Inc.
ChristianLivingBooks.com
We bring your dreams to fruition.

ISBN 9781562295981

Endorsements

"As a past client of Pastor Featherstone and a person of faith, I found his book both enlightening and inspiring. His innovative analogy between FICO scores and faith provides profound insights, making complex concepts accessible and relatable. Pastor Donnie's personal journey serves as a compelling example of how faith and financial principles can intersect to enrich one's life. This book clearly outlines a practical path to deepening one's relationship with the Lord while managing life's practicalities. It's a must-read for anyone seeking to harmonize their spiritual and financial well-being."

—Dr. Maurine B. Heard, MD
Anesthesiologist in Oakland, CA

"I'm proud of my brother Donnie Featherstone for bringing this powerful book to the world, but I'm not surprised. That's who he is—someone who empowers and encourages everyone he meets, and this book does just that. Having excellent credit scores is essential not only for residents of the United States but also for individuals in many other countries. While a decent credit score can open up a range of opportunities across various business sectors, an excellent credit score can accelerate success in these sectors even faster. This book provides a clear and actionable guide for improving one's credit score, with practical insights applicable to both FICO scores and general credit management. As a friend and former coworker, I have had the privilege of watching Donnie openly and proudly embrace his role as a preacher and pastor—the Loan Officer with a Conscience. His dedication to his work and his commitment to empowering and encouraging others is truly remarkable. This book does just that—empowers and encourages readers to enhance their credit scores and achieve their financial goals. I highly recommend it to anyone looking to understand and improve their earthly and heavenly credit scores."

—Edirisooriya Suranga (Ed)
KW East Bay
Keller Williams Realty
Realtor® | DRE #02187575

"This book is excellent for anyone looking to improve their credit scores, especially if you're considering buying a home or for those wanting to strengthen their spiritual connection. I first connected with Donnie in 2004 when we worked at the same mortgage company. He was already one of the top performers, known for his effective strategies in helping clients achieve their best. After reading his book, it's clear he hasn't lost his touch. I highly recommend this book to anyone aiming to boost their spiritual credit scores."

—Parti Pathmanathan
Broker, North American Financial, Inc.
NMLS #283103

"With decades of experience as a Real Estate Broker and Minister of the Gospel of Jesus Christ, I wholeheartedly endorse the author's expertise. Through distinct strategies, the reader is guided toward enhancing their spiritual and financial well-being. The narrative captivates from the outset, weaving a tapestry that engages the reader; I found the Humpty Dumpty allegory particularly resonant. Seamlessly integrating this tale with biblical wisdom, the author compellingly underscores the significance of embracing Christ, warning against the pitfalls of a life devoid of His presence."

—Rev. Joe L. Fisher
Fisher Realtors, Broker #01070856

"Pastor Donnie Featherstone masterfully weaves his expertise in the financial industry and his rich evangelical heritage to create a truly inspiring and practical guide for Christians seeking to deepen their spiritual walk with the Lord. This book is a must-read for anyone who desires to take their spiritual journey to the next level and experience the fullness of God's love and favor in their lives."

—Mother Ada Stevens, Supervisor of Women
California West Coast Ecclesiastical Jurisdiction, COGIC, Inc.

"This intellectually engaging book encourages readers to explore the depths of salvation's complexities. Pastor Featherstone's profound insights ignite a renewed purpose, encouraging us to embrace life with newfound energy and view our path with clarity. As a Bishop within the Lord's church, I've been personally challenged by the FICO score analogy to exceed mere mediocrity. My heartfelt gratitude goes to Pastor Featherstone for sharing these invaluable teachings. This book is indispensable, an essential addition to any library."

—Bishop Anthony L. Willis
Chief Apostle, Pure Ministries International Fellowship, Oakland, CA
Senior Pastor, Lily of the Valley Christian Center, Oakland, CA

"Pastor Featherstone has authored a highly relevant book that provides practical, biblical solutions to the everyday challenges we face in life. This book is a powerful educational resource, rich with the Word of God and filled with straightforward, easily implementable examples. Whether you're a new believer or a seasoned Christian, this book will undoubtedly help you grow in your faith and navigate life's ups and downs with greater clarity, confidence, and trust in God's plan for your life.

—Bishop Robert (Bob) Jackson, Senior Pastor
Acts Full Gospel Church, Oakland, CA
Prelate of California West Coast Ecclesiastical Jurisdiction
COGIC, Inc.

Table of Contents

Foreword

In a world often consumed by earthly pursuits and material measurements, it's both refreshing and profound to encounter a book that dares to explore a different kind of scorecard—one that transcends the tangible and delves into the realm of the eternal. *10 Keys to Maximizing Your Heavenly FICO SCORES* is precisely such a book.

Within these pages, the author invites us to consider a currency of greater significance—the currency of our souls. Grounded in the eternal wisdom of the Word of God, this book challenges us to assess our lives not merely by the wealth we amass or the accolades we earn but by the depth of our character, the sincerity of our faith, and the extent to which we live out the values of love, compassion, and service through and in Christ.

What sets this book apart is its unwavering commitment to truth. With candor and compassion, the author confronts human frailty and the inevitability of failure yet offers a message of hope and redemption that resounds with grace. Through personal anecdotes, biblical insights, and practical wisdom, readers are encouraged to embark on a journey of self-discovery. This journey leads not to perfection but to progress and transformation.

As a brother and a son, a teacher and a preacher, a pastor and now a bishop, and a husband who became a father and now a grandfather—I have had the privilege of witnessing firsthand the transformative power of faith in countless lives. Pastor Featherstone captures this truth with

1

eloquence and passion, offering a roadmap for anyone seeking to align their lives with the eternal values of God's kingdom through insight, sacrifice, and discipline.

This book also addresses the critical need for balance in our spiritual and financial lives. In a society where material success is often prioritized over spiritual well-being, Pastor Featherstone provides a refreshing perspective that integrates both aspects harmoniously. By emphasizing that true prosperity is not merely about financial wealth but also about spiritual richness, he invites us to pursue a holistic approach to life that honors God in all areas.

Moreover, this book offers practical advice for navigating the complexities of modern life. Whether dealing with financial challenges, personal crises, or spiritual dilemmas, the principles outlined provide a solid foundation for making wise decisions and maintaining a steadfast faith. The author's insights are deeply rooted in scripture and enriched by extensive experience as a pastor and senior home lending advisor.

The emphasis on character development throughout this book is particularly striking. In a time when external achievements and social validation are often prioritized, this book calls us back to the fundamentals of our faith—integrity, humility, and unwavering commitment to God's principles. It is a timely reminder that our true worth is measured by our alignment with divine values.

This book offers a deeply relatable and impactful guide through personal anecdotes, biblical insights, practical wisdom, and the author's experiences. These personal experiences lend authenticity and depth to the lessons, making the journey of faith and financial stewardship more tangible and achievable.

The practical steps outlined for each key ensure this book is both accessible and actionable, catering to readers from diverse backgrounds.

Whether you're a seasoned believer, a spiritual seeker, or simply curious about faith, these keys offer valuable insights and tools to deepen your faith and improve your financial stewardship. This book encourages a reassessment of priorities, a realignment of perspectives, and a commitment to living with eternal purpose. As you explore these pages, may you find inspiration and courage to pursue your journey toward heavenly FICO SCORES—valued not in monetary terms but in the virtues of love, faith, and grace. Let this guide lead you to a deeper connection with Christ and a more fulfilling pursuit of spiritual victory.

In conclusion, *10 Keys to Maximizing Your Heavenly FICO SCORES* is more than just a book; it is a call to action. It invites us to embark on a transformative journey that promises to enhance our spiritual and financial well-being and deepen our relationship with God. As you immerse yourself in its teachings, may you be inspired to live a life that reflects the eternal values of God's kingdom, marked by faith, integrity, and a commitment to excellence.

—J. Drew Sheard
Presiding Bishop & Chief Apostle
The Church of God in Christ, Inc.
Memphis, TN

Preface

Donnie Featherstone and I have been friends and colleagues, serving as pastors in the Gospel of Jesus Christ and within the Church of God in Christ Incorporated for three decades. Pastor Featherstone is also a Home Lending Advisor at Chase Bank, where he assists individuals in securing their financial homes and investments. As a pastor, he helps people secure their eternal home after they leave this earth.

Pastor Featherstone has been a visionary leader, aiding our communities in accessing both spiritual and economic resources to live the abundant life that our Lord Jesus Christ promised in His teachings. In the religious world, there is often an imbalanced ideology concerning the pursuit of spirituality alongside the attainment of financial wealth and economic security. For many Christians, this has been a persistent challenge due to the lack of balanced concepts that provide a healthy harmony between the heavenly and the earthly. As Dr. Martin Luther King, Jr. once remarked in his sermon "A Knock at Midnight," "Some churches freeze up, and some churches burn up!"

Pastor Featherstone imparts practical wisdom on living abundantly in both secular and spiritual spheres. His extensive success in the financial lending industry has endowed him with the expertise to guide individuals on when to purchase, hold, or sell. This unique combination of skills has allowed him to not only uplift the spiritual well-being of our communities but also to emerge as a leader in wealth-building through homeownership. His considerable experience as a lending specialist, not only in the Bay Area but across the nation, is highly regarded in the financial sector.

Pastor Featherstone explores how the 10 keys outlined in this book are crucial to achieving a life that honors God while also providing material prosperity. These principles, carefully woven into the fabric of this book, offer a roadmap to not only enhancing your spiritual journey but also your financial stability.

Each chapter delves into these core values, presenting practical steps and spiritual insights that guide readers toward a balanced life.

As you read this book, you will gain valuable insights into enhancing your financial portfolio through Pastor Featherstone's principles of success. You will also be inspired to see how faith can help you build not only a spiritual life filled with joy and peace but also a growing financial portfolio based on the principles revealed within. This book is a testament to the fact that true prosperity is a harmonious blend of spiritual and material wealth, achieved through diligent application of God-given principles.

Through his dual roles as a pastor and a senior home lending advisor, Pastor Featherstone has demonstrated that it is possible to live a life that honors God while also achieving financial success. His teachings challenge the traditional dichotomy between faith and finance, showing that they can and should complement each other. This holistic approach is not only innovative but also essential in today's world, where individuals often struggle to balance their spiritual and material pursuits.

I invite you to embark on this journey with an open heart and mind, ready to embrace the transformative power of these 10 keys. May this book serve as a beacon of hope and a source of practical guidance, helping you to maximize your heavenly FICO scores and live a life of true abundance.

—Dr. Yaahn G. Hunter Sr., Th.D.
Founder and Pastor of New Faith Cathedral COGIC, Vallejo, CA
Dean of Christian Education, California Northern First Jurisdiction
Church of God in Christ, Inc.

Understanding
the Value of This Book

In a sea of financial advice and self-help books, *10 Keys to Maximizing Your Heavenly FICO SCORES* stands out by offering a unique blend of practical strategies and spiritual principles. Unlike resources that focus solely on financial metrics, this book integrates spiritual values to provide a deeper approach to achieving both divine and earthly prosperity. By aligning financial practices with spiritual growth, it offers a holistic path to wealth and fulfillment and unlocks the path to prosperity.

What Sets This Book Apart from Others?

By implementing the spiritual principles behind maximizing your heavenly FICO SCORES, you can unlock both divine and earthly wealth and prosperity. This is achievable only through the 10 keys outlined in this book.

Question #1: What unique opportunity does this book offer you?

This book offers the reader a unique approach that combines spiritual and practical principles to enhance both divine and earthly prosperity. Unlike conventional financial guides, it integrates faith-based teachings with actionable steps to improve our overall well-being. Additionally, it provides practical lessons that we can incorporate into our daily lives, making it accessible and effective.

Question #2: How does this book fulfill your deepest desires?

Those who desire a holistic approach to prosperity that goes beyond material wealth, encompassing spiritual fulfillment and financial stability. This book addresses both aspects, providing the reader with a path to a more abundant and balanced life.

Question #3: How do the 10 keys serve as a framework for the reader's prosperity?

The 10 keys offer a structured framework that guides you through essential principles. These keys work synergistically to unlock prosperity in all areas of your life.

Question #4: How does this book differentiate itself from other financial or spiritual guides?

This book sets itself apart by uniquely blending financial wisdom with spiritual insights to create a comprehensive roadmap to prosperity. It underscores the critical importance of aligning financial practices with spiritual values, distinguishing it as a powerful and unique resource.

Question #5: Why should we trust the methods in this book?

The principles outlined in this book are backed by biblical teachings and practical experience. Over the course of my 26 years in the lending field and 22 years of pastoring, I have been teaching these principles, which are deeply rooted in biblical passages. Personally, I applied these principles to rebuild my own credit after filing for bankruptcy in 2010 following the housing meltdown. Many clients and church members have experienced transformative financial and spiritual growth through these teachings. Remarkably, numerous clients were so impacted by their experience that they became members of my ministry, underscoring the profound effect of these methods. The consistent, positive feedback and personal stories shared by those who have benefited from these principles provide compelling evidence of their effectiveness.

Question #6: What benefits can I expect from following the 10 keys?

By following the 10 keys, you can expect enhanced financial stability, deeper spiritual fulfillment, and a more balanced approach to life. Tangible benefits include improved financial health, while intangible benefits encompass greater peace of mind, a stronger sense of purpose, and alignment with spiritual values.

Question #7: How are the 10 keys practically applied?

Each key is based on a specific principle and provides actionable steps and practical advice for implementation. For example, "Faith that Moves God" teaches how to cultivate faith that influences divine intervention, while "Protect Your Identity" offers strategies to safeguard both spiritual and financial identity. Together, these keys form a comprehensive approach to achieving prosperity. Each chapter delves deeper and uncovers additional principles, offering more insights and discoveries that guide you on your journey to financial and spiritual growth.

Question #8: What support is available if I have questions or need help?

A variety of support systems are available to assist you. A workbook is available to provide further practical assistance. You can also join online communities, participate in workshops, and take advantage of personal coaching services. Additionally, credit repair guidance will be coming soon. For more personalized support and additional resources, you can reach out through the author's website.

Question #9: What challenges might be encountered, and how can they be overcome?

While the principles in this book are designed to be universally applicable, changing long-standing habits or mindsets can be challenging. However, these challenges can be overcome with persistence. This book helps readers renew their minds and prepare for new opportunities. With dedication and determination, these obstacles can be conquered, leading to significant personal and financial growth.

Question #10: What should I do first to start applying the principles?
The first step is to read the introduction and the first chapter to grasp the foundational principles. Start by engaging with the reflections provided in these sections. This will set the stage for a transformative journey through the remaining keys, equipping you with the insights and tools needed to achieve both financial and spiritual growth.

Introduction

My purpose in writing this book is to fortify the faith of every believer, transcending the boundaries of race, ethnicity, age, gender, and socioeconomic status. By restoring minds and equipping nations with truth, I aim to empower God's people to triumph over the enemy's schemes. By sharing these insights, the goal is to bring people together and provide them with the tools they need to live victorious and purposeful lives in an ever-changing world. This book aims to be a guide for everyone, offering practical biblical solutions to life's everyday challenges.

Allow me to start with complete transparency. The information presented in this book is entirely the work of a ghostwriter—my Guide and Comforter, the Holy Ghost. I do not know everything on this subject matter, but He does and has commissioned me to share how easy it is for any of us to maximize our heavenly FICO SCORES. No matter what our current ratings are, we can continually improve them. The Holy Ghost could have chosen any of you to share this information. I am grateful to be deputized in His army to get this next-level information to His people and be the voice of one speaking the truth in this time of misinformation. The information provided is impactful, transformational, duplicatable, inspirational, revelational, and engaging.

God asked in Isaiah Chapter 6, "Whom shall I send, and who will go for me?" And just as Isaiah said, "Here I am; send me," I said, "Yes, Lord, here am I." So, He spoke it, and I wrote it. Hence, the birthing of *10 Keys to Maximizing Your Heavenly FICO SCORES*. If you are willing to follow and apply all the steps, the Comforter guarantees you will not just raise but maximize your heavenly FICO SCORES.

The apostle Paul comes to mind. Before his conversion, he was known as Saul in Hebrew, meaning (prayed for) the saint slayer, the crusher of the faith, and the grim reaper, as he hauled God's people off to jail and witnessed them being stoned. This lowered his heavenly SCORES to 300. After his conversion, he was called Paul by his Greek name, which means small or humble. He went from hauling God's people off to jail to becoming a defender of the faith, the Apostle to the Gentiles, a church planter, a mentor to God's people, and an author of 13 books in the New Testament, 14 if you give him credit for Hebrews. He turned his credit rating around and maximized his heavenly SCORES to 850 as he fought the good fight of faith to the end.

The number 10 is also significant to the FICO SCORES Acrostic of 10 letters as each letter forms our 10 chapters for this book as well as the workbook. Understanding the universal and historical importance of the number 10 can deepen our appreciation of its role in structuring our approach to maximizing your heavenly FICO SCORES.

Before delving into FICO Scores, it is essential to recognize the profound significance of the number 10. This number holds deep meaning across various contexts, including the Bible, cultural traditions, and numerology.

Biblical Significance

In the Bible, the number 10 represents commandments, completeness, order, divine authority, tithing, trials, and testing.

- **The Ten Commandments**: These are the foundational laws given by God to Moses on Mount Sinai (Exodus 20:3-17), forming the bedrock of Judaism and Christianity.

- **Completeness of Divine Order**: Biblically, 10 signifies the completion of God's order. This is evident in the 10 generations from Adam to Noah and from Noah to Abraham, marking spans of divine completeness.

- **Tithing**: Instituted before the law, tithing is demonstrated by Abraham giving a tenth of everything to Melchizedek (Hebrews 7:1-7). This act symbolizes faith and devotion (Leviticus 27:30-32).

- **Testing**: God sent 10 plagues to test Pharaoh's resolve and free His people (Exodus chapters 7-12).

- **Proving**: Daniel, Hananiah, Mishael, and Azariah requested a 10-day diet of vegetables and water, proving to be healthier than those who ate from the king's table (Daniel 1:11-16).

Cultural Foundational Significance

In Western and Chinese culture, along with ancient Egyptian, Greek, and Indian cultures, the number 10 is the foundation of all counting and a pivotal point in numerology. It symbolizes a return to unity and the end of a cycle. These examples show that 10 is universally recognized as a fundamental building block in numerology and counting systems.

- **Decades**: A period of 10 years often marks significant cultural or historical milestones.

- **Top 10 Lists**: Common in media and entertainment, top 10 lists highlight the most notable items in a category, emphasizing the importance of ranking within a structure of 10.

- **Completeness and Perfection**: The number 10 symbolizes completeness or perfection. It is the base of the decimal system, fundamental in mathematics and human life. Our anatomy typically features 10 fingers and 10 toes, underscoring its association with basic counting.

Numerology and Symbolism in Various Religions

- **Pythagorean Tradition**: The number 10 is seen as perfect, containing the sum of the first four numbers (1+2+3+4=10), representing unity, duality, harmony, and completion.

- **Hinduism**: The number 10 signifies completeness and totality, often depicted by deities with ten arms representing their power.

What Is FICO?

FICO, a trademark of Fair Isaac Corporation, is a cornerstone in the realm of credit scoring. Established in 1956 by Bill Fair and Earl Isaac, Fair Isaac Corporation is a data analytics powerhouse headquartered in Bozeman, Montana. FICO scores have become a global standard for assessing consumer credit risk, integral to lending decisions both in the United States and across the globe. Countries such as Canada, the United Kingdom, Australia, India, South Africa, Mexico, and New Zealand have adopted FICO scores, tailoring their use to comply with local financial regulations and practices. These scores are derived from data collected by major credit reporting agencies, including Experian, Equifax, and TransUnion. Lenders leverage FICO scores alongside additional credit report information to evaluate credit risk, ensuring informed decisions in extending credit.

With over two and a half decades in the home lending industry and thirty-two years spent proclaiming the gospel of Jesus Christ, I have come to understand the immense power of trusting and relying on the Savior's thoughts. I've been a private client and senior home lending advisor for a major financial institution for many years. I've assisted over 3,000 clients in purchasing new homes and refinancing existing home loans. Like many individuals I've assisted, there were tens of thousands of prospects I couldn't help due to their CIA: Credit, Income, Assets, and D: Debt. In the marketplace, I'm recognized as a loan officer with a conscience. You can find more about me by googling Donnie Featherstone Chase Lending. As a home lending advisor, I help people secure their homes all around the country. As a pastor, I've assisted people in securing their eternal homes after departing Earth, though I'm not sure of the number.

When understanding how our credit scores are determined, we must recognize that not all factors carry equal weight. The credit scoring models used by FICO and other agencies assign specific values to different aspects of our credit history, and understanding these weights can help us prioritize our efforts to improve our scores. Let's take a closer look at the breakdown of these factors and their relative importance in the overall credit assessment process.

Weight of Factors in Credit Assessment

Payment History – 35 percent

Amounts You Owe – 30 percent

Length of Your Credit History – 15 percent

New Credit You Apply For – 10 percent

Types of Credit You Use – 10 percent

Excellent credit is always ideal, but good credit scores can be hit or miss, depending on the lender. You can expect much higher interest rates if you have fair credit scores and are approved. On the other hand, if your credit scores are poor or low, you will be denied credit regardless of your ethnicity, race, sex, or age. In this book, we will explore the concept of heavenly FICO SCORES:

The Acrostic for FICO SCORES

F – Faith

I – Identity

C – Commitment

O – Obedience

S – Sanctification

C – Change

O – Obligation

R – Righteousness

E – Excel

S – Stewardship

Faith, obedience, and stewardship can improve your spiritual credit. By applying these principles, you will draw closer to God and experience the abundant life He has planned for you.

Much like FICO scores, the quality of our connection with God influences how swiftly our prayers are answered. An excellent credit/relationship with Him means prayers are answered quickly. A good credit/relationship moves God but not as quickly as excellent credit does. A fair credit/relationship is hit or miss. And if you have a bad credit/relationship with God? Good luck with that one; you may want someone else with an excellent relationship to intercede on your behalf.

Are your prayers not being answered? Check your heavenly credit! Has someone in the family ruined their credit and asked you to co-sign a loan? First off, you should never co-sign for anyone. But let's say you do, and unfortunately, you have not monitored your credit. Now, you have been declined as well due to poor credit scores. This happened to me years ago. Embarrassing! It's time to monitor, review, rebuild, and renew our heavenly credit SCORES daily.

Someone calls with a prayer request, trusting in your seemingly strong relationship with God. However, they don't know you haven't been praying regularly due to life's issues. You haven't fasted in months and only read your Bible during Bible study. Consequently, your prayers aren't answered either. How shameful. Sadly, this has happened to me as well.

Most of our heavenly relationships are subpar despite the many years we have been believers. We've been in a relationship with God all these years, but most of our heavenly relationships are subpar due to a lack of daily communication with the heavenly Father. We do not pray or miss a meal. We forget about reading, let alone studying the Word of God. People come to us because we always talk about Jesus and attend church services regularly, but our relationships with Him are below standard. I would prefer to have excellent credit and not require it than to have poor credit and be unable to use it when necessary. Similarly, having an excellent relationship with God is great, so when you call upon Him, He responds. However, it shouldn't be surprising if you call on God without a covenant relationship and He doesn't answer.

Your FICO score can prevent you from getting that new job, a promotion, approval for a car loan, a home loan, and a great interest rate. Your heavenly FICO SCORES can prevent you from having the blessings that God wants to give you.

As you read and apply the principles outlined in this book, you will find the tools to repair, rebuild, maintain, and over time maximize your heavenly FICO SCORES with God. Regardless of where you find yourself on your spiritual journey, if you are ready to elevate your heavenly FICO SCORES and experience the abundance of God's blessings, I invite you to embark on this transformative journey with me. Within these pages, you will discover practical guidance and encouragement to support you every step of the way.

Chapter 1

Faith That Moves God

You may or may not agree with me, and that's fine. But can we agree to disagree? This might hurt and upset you, but please listen to my honest opinion. Faith and gambling are similar, but they are not the same. Gambling does not, cannot, and will not ever reach the threshold of faith. Consider this: whenever people drive motor vehicles without a driver's license, insurance, or registration, they are breaking the law and taking risks, hoping they won't be caught by law enforcement. This person is gambling.

Similarly, living without health insurance, life insurance, renter's insurance, homeowner's insurance, or burial insurance is also a gamble. You are essentially betting that you won't get sick, die, or experience any incidents at your residence. However, if these things happen, you will regret that gamble.

Some might say they have faith, believing that nothing will ever happen that would require them to need insurance. But my friend, that is the epitome of gamblers, those so immature, unprepared, and plain selfish that they leave their fate in the hands of others. It's irresponsible to expect someone else to take care of what you refuse to do.

While faith and gambling may seem to share some similarities on the surface, they are fundamentally different at their core. Gambling relies on chance and luck, while faith is based on trust in God and His promises. True faith requires obedience and action, not just wishful thinking.

Unfortunately, sometimes we break the law, live negligently, bend the rules, operate in the gray, or embellish on our taxes. People carry legal and illegal weapons for their protection, claiming they are doing it by faith. You are gambling. If you do not live in a constitutional carry state or have a concealed carry weapons permit, you are gambling.

The Bible warns us in James 1:13-15, "Let no man say when he is tempted, I am tempted of God: for God cannot be tempted with evil, neither tempteth he any man: But every man is tempted, when he is drawn away of his own lust, and enticed. Then when lust hath conceived, it bringeth forth sin: and sin, when it is finished, bringeth forth death."

Addicted to Faith

How could a Holy God allow us to operate below His standards by breaking the law, being negligent, irresponsible, selfish, and lazy, and then call it faith? That plan is simply a gamble. Sad to say, millions of Americans have gambling problems or addictions to any number of things: food, drugs, alcohol, sex, pornography, smoking, work, and the list goes on and on. But rarely is anyone addicted to faith.

Think about it: we spend our entire lives being addicted to these things, only to come to Christ and not be addicted to Him. What a tragic irony that the very thing that can make us free—an all-consuming faith in God—is so often neglected while destructive addictions are allowed to rule.

All of us should become addicted to faith in God, but most people leave their future up to fate, not faith. When we hear the seemingly absurd things required of faith, we retreat to our posture of, "That sounds crazy" or "I don't think that will work." Like Naaman, the leper in 2 Kings 5:14, we don't want to take seven dips in the muddy pond of

Jordan. We don't believe like the widow in 2 Kings 4:1-7, who was told to borrow many vessels, shut the door, pour out until full, pay off her debts, and then live off the rest. How crazy is it to be thrown in the lion's den and use them as pillows? What about being cast into a fiery furnace and coming out not even smelling or looking like what you have been through?

These biblical examples demonstrate the radical nature of true faith. While it often seems foolish or illogical to human reasoning, genuine faith trusts God's wisdom above our limited understanding.

Let's rebuild our heavenly FICO SCORES with faith. So, where do we begin? By having faith in God.

Without faith in God, it's all a gamble.

Faith in God is powerful; it's how we were saved—through faith. The *Oxford English Dictionary* defines faith as complete trust or confidence in someone or something. Years ago, God gave me an acronym for TRUST: Totally Rely Upon the Savior's Thoughts.

> *"For I know the thoughts that I think toward you, saith the LORD, thoughts of peace, and not of evil, to give you an expected end." (Jeremiah 29:11)*

Whenever you see the word "thoughts" in the Bible, replace it with "plans." God has a plan for His people, so we, His people, must trust and believe, even when we don't know what the plan holds. Faith is the manifestation of God through Jesus Christ and the work He did on the cross.

"For God so loved the world, that he gave his only begotten Son, that whosoever believeth in him should not perish, but have everlasting life." (John 3:16)

Faith does not end with what Christ did on the cross; that's where it begins. Faith continues. It starts as a tiny mustard seed but grows into a giant tree where birds can find food and shelter. It may start weakly, but if activated, it will become strong.

Unfortunately, faith is on life support for most Christians due to situations and circumstances that have diluted, polluted, and clouded our belief in God. But we must remember that situations and circumstances are chances for His strength to become perfect in our weakness. Instead of yielding to skepticism and doubt, we must cling to the faith that sustained our forefathers, fueled their endurance through trials, and brought them through victoriously.

They sang songs like "We've Come This Far by Faith" and "Through it all, I learned to trust in Jesus, I learned to trust in God." Remember to Totally Rely Upon the Savior's Thoughts. Trust God's thoughts only. You see, it's all for God, or it's all for nothing! So, whatever you face, singing denotes to doubt that you will not be defeated, as you are addicted to faith, and this too shall pass.

Every Day Faith
We unconsciously use faith without even realizing it: when we sit in our favorite chairs, put the key in the door lock, start our cars, board public transportation, and work for 40 hours. Our subconscious tells us the chair will hold, the key will open the lock, the vehicle will start, public transportation will get us to our destinations, and the job will pay. We don't think about it; we just do it. If we want to please God and see our heavenly FICO SCORES elevated, it starts with faith in God.

"Cast not away therefore your confidence, which hath great recompense of reward. Now the just shall live by faith: but if any man draw back, my soul shall have no pleasure in him. But we are not of them who draw back unto perdition; but of them that believe to the saving of the soul." (Hebrews 10:35, 38-39)

> ## We unconsciously use faith without even realizing it.

Don't toss away your confidence; it will bring great rewards. The first way the just, also called the righteous, begin to raise their scores is to live by faith. However, once we start to doubt, our scores dip. Nevertheless, we must not retreat to our old ways but hold onto faith in the deliverance of our souls. We have all sinned and fallen short of God's glory. Don't practice going backward. If you fall, confess your sins because God is faithful and just to deliver you.

My late pastor Archie Brice would say: "If you fall, don't lay there but get up and dust yourself off." In other words, repent and keep going forward. This leads us to Hebrews 11:1, "Now faith is the substance of things hoped for, the evidence of things not seen."

Present faith is material matter, proof of the things we hope for. It is the title deed to prove we have things we do not see. Now faith confirms I have it before I see it.

"Through faith we understand that the worlds were framed by the word of God, so that things which are seen were not made of things which do appear." (Hebrews 11:3)

In faith, we can understand how God used His Word to create the world, bringing things seen from what is not visible into existence. God thought it, spoke it, and the Holy Spirit manifested it.

> *"But without faith it is impossible to please him: for he that cometh to God must believe that he is, and that he is a rewarder of them that diligently seek him." (Hebrews 11:6)*

Being void of faith, makes pleasing God unattainable. Anyone who approaches God must believe that He is and that He is a compensator to all who purposefully seek Him. We must believe God by seeing all He is and all He did without physically seeing Him.

The Tale of Humpty Dumpty

Have you heard the nursery rhyme about Humpty Dumpty? It is an English riddle portraying a human-like egg, though he is not an egg. It goes:

> *Humpty Dumpty sat on a wall.*
> *Humpty Dumpty had a great fall.*
> *All the king's horses and all the king's men*
> *Couldn't put Humpty together again.*

What does this nursery rhyme mean? The *Oxford English Dictionary* states there are theories about the meaning of *Humpty Dumpty*. Some historians believe *Humpty Dumpty* was just a riddle about breakable things. Others suggest that Humpty Dumpty is King Richard III of England, who is supposed to have been humpbacked and who was defeated at the Battle of Bosworth Field in 1485.

The metaphor was that Humpty is the King; the wall is his reign and fight to preserve power. The fall is his defeat and "All the king's horses and all the king's men" are the army that failed to prevail.

Another theory is that Humpty is a cannon. During the English Civil War, history tells us of a one-eyed gunner named Thompson who managed to position a cannon named "Humpty Dumpty" at the top of the tower of St. Mary's Church. From this vantage point, he inflicted untold destruction. However, return cannon fire eventually dislodged both Thompson and the cannon, leading to their downfall. Hence, the phrase "had a great fall" may have originated from this event.

Humpty lost focus and balance and then fell off the wall and cracked into pieces. When people lose focus on faith, they will have a great fall. The world did not have what Humpty needed to make him whole. In the same way, the world also does not have what you need to be made whole. Too bad Humpty never met Jesus. When you try to do anything without Christ, it won't last. Remember, it's not by power or might but by the Spirit of the Lord.

We must be careful not to allow people, circumstances, or anything else to become such an unhealthy fixation that it pulls our attention away from Christ. Keeping our eyes firmly fixed on Jesus is pivotal to living by faith. When we take our eyes off Him, even momentarily, we are in danger of stumbling and falling like Humpty Dumpty.

The world will constantly try to divert our focus onto lesser things—wealth, status, pleasures, and the approval of others. But we cannot afford to have our faith disrupted by such distractions. True transformation can only occur when we firmly set our minds on the Lord, shutting out the noise and removing any idols that compete for our devotion. Let us be like Isaiah, having our spiritual eyes opened to the glories of the Almighty through unwavering faith. Faith is the bedrock of the Christian life. Without it, we cannot please God or access the abundant life He has promised us.

Let us be like the great faith warriors of old who "through faith subdued kingdoms, worked righteousness, obtained promises, stopped the mouths of lions, quenched the violence of fire" (Hebrews 11:33-34). Let us approach each day, each circumstance, with a bold, audacious faith that declares, "I will not fear, for You are with me" (Isaiah 41:10). As we live by faith in the Son of God, we honor God and rebuild our heavenly FICO SCORES.

In the end, faith is simply taking God at His Word and ordering our steps accordingly, no matter how foolish it may seem to the world. May we all become so addicted to faith that the world marvels at the exploits accomplished through our unwavering trust in Christ. Indeed, the just shall live by faith, which overcomes the world and ushers us into eternal glories.

CHAPTER 2

Distinct Identity

Identity is the essence of our character and habits and plays a crucial role in our spiritual journey. Our character and habits shape our thoughts, actions, relationships, and relationship with God. In a world that often tries to define us by our circumstances, failures, or the opinions of others, it's essential to understand that our true identity is found in Christ.

This chapter will explore what it means to have a distinct identity in God and how embracing it can lead to a more fulfilling life and higher heavenly FICO SCORES. We'll examine the importance of having a good name, living a life of integrity, and allowing God to define who we are rather than the world around us.

Identity is the state of being who or what a person or thing is. We were created male and female. However, today, a person can choose not to identify with either gender and be non-binary. I'll stop there—that's not the purpose of this book.

> *"A good name is rather to be chosen than great riches, and loving favour rather than silver and gold." (Proverbs 22:1)*

Your name is just as valuable as material wealth. Know your identity! Protect you identity! Improve your identity!

For God's will to be done on Earth as it is in Heaven, He created us in His image and likeness so we could have dominion over ourselves and Earth. It is our responsibility to defend and protect our identity from scammers, thieves, hackers, con artists, phishing schemes, shysters, pickpockets, muggers, and anyone else daring enough to attempt to attack and destroy our lives. We must take extra precautions with our identity by constantly monitoring our surroundings, identity, credit reports, credit freezes, passwords, security questions, etc.

Our identity is ours alone to build, maintain, protect, and make great, despite the culture, new beliefs, values, and personality of a very liberal or conservative society, depending on where you live. When was the last time you checked your credit rating with God? Is it poor, fair, good, or excellent? Just because you avoid checking doesn't make it better. When you least expect it, you may need FICO scores for a car, personal loan, or God to answer an emergency prayer request. So, it pays to know where our FICO scores stand, both earthly and heavenly. FICO knows our DOB and SSN and rates you 300-850, continually moving. God is a Spirit and knows our DNA by how we worship Him in spirit and truth. The more we worship, the higher our heavenly FICO SCORES increase.

> **Our identity is ours alone to build, maintain, protect, and make great.**

Identical Twins

Let's look at identical twins. They are rarely entirely identical. Their skin tone, weight, height, and even personality, to name a few characteristics, can be different. How does this happen? A single egg, once fertilized by a single sperm, divides into two cells. Identical twins have the same DNA but may not look identical because of environmental factors such as position in the womb and life experiences after birth. A study of 381 pairs of identical twins and two sets of identical triplets found that only 38 were genetically identical, as Tina Hesman Saey for *Science News* reported. Most had just a few points of genetic mismatch, but 39 had more than 100 differences in their DNA (Study from Jan 13, 2021).

Just because it looks like a duck/FICO SCORES and sounds like a duck/FICO SCORES doesn't mean it's a great quacking duck/FICO SCORES. It could be a doppelgänger, a person who looks like another person and could, in fact, be a body double for them. However, they are not related. Stay on top of your ducks, your FICO SCORES, and your relationship of worshiping God in spirit and truth to maximize your heavenly SCORES.

Today, more people wear hoodies over their heads, even when it's warm outside. This makes it difficult to identify them when approaching from behind. The reason for this trend is unclear. Perhaps it could be a bad hair day? But I'm not judging. Additionally, I've seen more reckless drivers with dark-tinted windows compared to those without. These drivers are more emboldened, often cutting you off in traffic, as their identities are concealed. Unfortunately, this behavior has become a norm.

Identity Theft

No business or person can trust the other without overtly questioning the other party to confirm they are who they claim to be, whether in person, online, or over the phone. Nowadays, while conducting business with identity theft at an all-time high, everyone is extremely cautious due to scammers using phishing schemes. To ensure that you don't become a victim of identity theft, you must do your due diligence and know to whom you're speaking: their full name, account number, last four digits of their SSN, security code, and PIN. If someone contacts you claiming to be from a company you do business with, tell them you'll call them back through official channels and verify before giving any information that could be used to steal your identity. Many will say they represent a company without actually being with the company, trying to deceive you into sending money before they can help you. Guard your identity, your accounts, and your personal information.

Identity theft has been around for centuries, dating back as far as the Bible in the Garden of Eden when Satan stole Adam and Eve's identity from God. Rebekah helped her son Jacob steal his twin brother Esau's identity.

Since the invention of the World Wide Web, this digital information platform has distributed even more misinformation loaded with scammers, phishing schemes, and conspiracy theories. They never sleep, constantly pushing their agendas and looking for new cons to rob you blind and steal your life's savings by selling you things that won't benefit or profit you. If it sounds too good to be true, such as getting rich quickly without putting in any effort, don't fall for it!

When someone knocks at your door, you should ask who it is before you open it while looking through the peephole to confirm. When your cell phone rings from an unknown or blocked caller, say hello and ask who's calling if you decide to answer. You need to protect your identity. Along with knowing, protecting, and improving your identity, you'd better find out whom you're dealing with before you fall victim to a scheme to defraud you of your life's savings.

If you were ever pulled over while driving, you know what happens: the officer will ask for your name, driver's license, insurance, and registration. With a Class C license, you can't drive a Class A or B vehicle—wrong identification. You'll be cited, and the car could be impounded.

Here is the DRF (Donnie R. Featherstone) interpretation of the story in Matthew 16:13. Jesus asked His disciples: "How do I identify with the people? Whom do they say I am?" The disciples said: "Some say You are John the Baptist; some say Elijah; others say Jeremiah; some say You make the best wine; You never send people away hungry; You are one of the prophets."

He said, "Okay, that's fine. I can see that. I expected as much; they have no relationship with Me. But you do. You've been following, listening, learning, seeing, fellowshipping, partnering, and eating with Me. Do you know My identity? Whom do *you* say I am? Do *you* know who I am?" None of them could answer. They were all speechless, with egg on their faces. But Peter got the memo from Heaven and said, "You are the Christ, the Son of the living God." We all need the same memo from Heaven. Despite what we're going through, never forget who God is and what He has already done for us; know who Christ is and our identity in Him. We can do all things through Christ who strengthens us.

> *"For we do not have a High Priest who cannot sympathize with our weaknesses, but was in all points tempted as we are, yet without sin. Let us therefore come boldly to the throne of grace, that we may obtain mercy and find grace to help in time of need."*
> *(Hebrews 4:15-16)*

The "S" on Our Chest

Jesus Christ, our high priest, knows precisely how our infirmities feel. He was tempted with issues like ours, yet He did not sin. He experienced situations that cause our flesh and eyes to lust and cause pride to rise in our emotions. So, let's boldly approach the throne of grace so that we may receive mercy and grace to help us in our time of need. In a nutshell, our relationship with Him, knowing our position in Him and our placement through Him, brings self-awareness of who we are because of Him.

When we surrender to His will for our lives, He reveals our true identity in Him. We receive keys to the kingdom of Heaven, so there's no longer a need to walk around acting like Clark Kent. We can take off our masks and show the world the "S" for Saved, the "S" for being a Saint, and the "S" for being Sound. Our identity in Christ is found in our relationship with Him.

Many identity thieves have tried to pretend they are from God. They are wolves in sheep's clothing, tares that resemble wheat, and goats postering as sheep. So, it is no great thing if Satan's ministers can transform into the ministers of righteousness. It's time to stop falling for the enemy's con game.

> *"The thief does not come except to steal, and to kill, and to destroy." (John 10:10)*

The enemy wants to steal your purpose, kill your influence, and destroy your reputation and life.

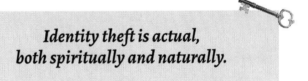

**Identity theft is actual,
both spiritually and naturally.**

Identity Crisis

The church, our government, the world, the economy, individuals, and even nature are going through an identity crisis. The church doesn't know if it wants to be the church or be like the world—an identity crisis. Our government is in turmoil—the left and right are fighting to control the identity of the nation. The world is filled with wars and rumors of more wars. Our economy is in crisis. We print money to support everyone and causes outside of the USA without dealing with our issues of poverty, social injustice, social economics, inequalities. overt disparities within our societies, as well as civil unrest, homelessness, a lack of resources in our communities, lack of opportunities, mass incarceration, sickness and disease, and the wealth gap. Charity begins at home and then spreads abroad. With the same effort we place into building regions in foreign countries, we should focus on our home, the USA.

We spend more time keeping up with the Joneses, trying to prove to people who we aren't instead of being who we are. We try to impress people who don't care about us. Our goal should not be to impress people by trying to look prosperous when we are broke and can't pay our bills on time. I heard a man on YouTube say, "I'd rather carry a plastic bag with $5,000.00 in it than carry a Louis Vuitton with $100.00 in it." Many people suffer from identity crises and care too much about what others think of them.

> *"When I was a child, I spoke as a child, I understood as a child, I thought as a child: but when I became a man, I put away childish things." (1 Corinthians 13:11)*

Stop trying to prove to others that you are something you aren't. Don't try to make people like you. People will never love me for who I am until I can love myself and learn my identity. If you can't be with the one you love, love the one you're with 24/7.

Who Is He to You?

We were created in God's image and His likeness. He gave us dominion. But we have surrendered it for someone's opinion. I'll take personal dominion over man's opinion of me anytime. Here are some names God used to identify Himself to His people:

- To Abraham, He was Jehovah Jireh, my provider; Jehovah Tsidkenu, our righteousness.

- To Moses, He was "I AM THAT I AM," Jehovah Rapha, my healer.

- To Ezekiel, He was a wheel in the middle of the wheel.

- To Amos, He was a plumbline.

- To Jeremiah, He was a battle axe.

- David said He was a rod and a staff.

- Gideon called Him Jehovah Shalom, my peace.

Some know Him as a Rock in a weary land. To others, He's a leaning post, a Way-maker, a Lily in the Valley, the Prince of Peace, and the Wonderful Counselor. He is my strength, my joy, and my all in all.

The Names of God

As we seek to understand and strengthen our identity in Christ, it's important to recognize the many facets of God's character and the countless ways He meets us in our times of need. Throughout the Bible, God reveals Himself through various names, each highlighting a specific attribute or aspect of His nature. By exploring these names, we gain a deeper appreciation for who God is and how He relates to us on a personal level. Let's take a look at some of the names of God from A to Z:

Abba (Mark 14:36)
Advocate (1 John 2:1)
Almighty (Revelation 1:8)
Alpha and Omega (Revelation 22:13)
Ancient of Days (Daniel 7:9)
Anointed One (Psalm 2:2)
Author of Eternal Salvation (Hebrews 5:9)
Author and Finisher of Our Faith (Hebrews 12:2)
Banner (Jehovah-Nissi) (Exodus 17:15)

Beginning and the End (Revelation 22:13)
Blessed and Only Potentate (1 Timothy 6:15)
Bread of Life (John 6:35)
Bridegroom (Matthew 9:15)
Bright Morning Star (Revelation 22:16)
Captain of Salvation (Hebrews 2:10)
Chief Cornerstone (Ephesians 2:20)
Christ (Matthew 16:16)
Comforter (John 14:16)
Creator (Isaiah 40:28)
Dayspring (Luke 1:78)
Deliverer (Romans 11:26)
Door (John 10:9)
Emmanuel/Immanuel (Matthew 1:23)
Eternal God (Deuteronomy 33:27)
Everlasting Father (Isaiah 9:6)
Exalted One (Isaiah 33:5)
Faithful and True (Revelation 19:11)
Father (Matthew 6:9)
First and Last (Revelation 1:17)
Fortress (Psalm 18:2)
Friend of Sinners (Matthew 11:19)
Good Shepherd (John 10:11)
Great High Priest (Hebrews 4:14)
Guide (Psalm 48:14)
Helper (Psalm 54:4)
Holy One (Isaiah 43:15)
Hope of Glory (Colossians 1:27)
Horn of Salvation (Luke 1:69)
I AM (Exodus 3:14)
Image of God (Colossians 1:15)

Jehovah (Exodus 6:3)

Jehovah-Jireh (The Lord Will Provide) (Genesis 22:14)

Jehovah-Rapha (The Lord Who Heals) (Exodus 15:26)

Jehovah-Shalom (The Lord Our Peace) (Judges 6:24)

Jehovah-Tsidkenu (The Lord Our Righteousness) (Jeremiah 23:6)

Jesus (Matthew 1:21)

Judge (Psalm 75:7)

King of Kings (Revelation 19:16)

King of Glory (Psalm 24:7-10)

King of the Ages (1 Timothy 1:17)

Lamb of God (John 1:29)

Last Adam (1 Corinthians 15:45)

Light of the World (John 8:12)

Lily in the Valley (Song of Solomon 2:2)

Lion of the Tribe of Judah (Revelation 5:5)

Living Water (John 4:10)

Lord of Lords (Revelation 19:16)

Lord of the Harvest (Matthew 9:38)

Lord Our Righteousness (Jeremiah 23:6)

Majestic Glory (2 Peter 1:17)

Man of Sorrows (Isaiah 53:3)

Mediator (1 Timothy 2:5)

Mighty God (Isaiah 9:6)

Name Above All Names (Philippians 2:9)

Nazarene (Matthew 2:23)

Only Begotten Son (John 3:16)

Our Hope (1 Timothy 1:1)

Our Peace (Ephesians 2:14)

Prince of Peace (Isaiah 9:6)

Prophet (Deuteronomy 18:15)

Purifier (Malachi 3:3)

Quieter of the Storm (Mark 4:39)
Redeemer (Job 19:25)
Refuge (Psalm 46:1)
Resurrection and the Life (John 11:25)
Righteous One (Acts 3:14)
Rock (1 Corinthians 10:4)
Rose of Sharon (Song of Solomon 2:1)
Root of David (Revelation 5:5)
Ruler (Matthew 2:6)
Savior (Luke 2:11)
Shield (Psalm 3:3)
Son of the Living God (Matthew 16:16)
Son of Man (Matthew 8:20)
Spirit of Truth (John 14:17)
Strong Tower (Proverbs 18:10)
Teacher (John 13:13)
True Vine
Unchanging (James 1:17)
Upholder of Justice (Hebrews 1:3)
Victory (1 Corinthians 15:57)
Vine (John 15:1)
Way (John 14:6)
Wonderful Counselor (Isaiah 9:6)
Word (John 1:1)
EXcellent (Psalm 8:1)
Yahweh-Yireh (The Lord Will Provide) (Psalms 23:1)
Zeal of the Lord (Isaiah 9:7)
Zion's King (Psalm 2:6)

Whatever you need from Him, whenever you need Him, He is there. We all identify with Him at different times, and He identifies with what we need. To someone, He is a bridge over troubled waters, a burden bearer, a lawyer in the courtroom. To others, He is a doctor in the sick room, bread when you're hungry, and water when you're thirsty. We all need Him to be something at some time, but we don't all need Him to be the same thing at the same time. He is our Redeemer. He identifies with whatever you need Him to be, so let's improve our identity before we need Him. So, when we call, we can find help in our time of need. Our heavenly SCORES continue to increase as we improve our identity with God.

CHAPTER 3

Next-Level Commitment

"Commit thy way unto the LORD; trust also in him; and he shall bring it to pass." (Psalm 37:5)

Commitment is the foundation upon which all successful relationships are built, whether they're with God or with others. Just as we expect loyalty, dedication, and unwavering support from our spouse, family, and friends, God expects us to be fully committed to Him and His will for our lives. He desires our wholehearted devotion, not a halfhearted or lukewarm approach to our faith.

One of the most significant challenges we face is learning how to remain committed despite the difficulties, heartaches, and setbacks that come our way. It is easy to start strong, enthusiastic, and determined, but it takes remarkable resilience to keep going when the road gets tough. We cannot allow the trials and tribulations of life to derail us from the path God has set before us. We must keep our eyes fixed on the prize and press on, knowing that He who began a good work in us will be faithful to complete it (Philippians 1:6).

"It is of the LORD'S mercies that we are not consumed, because his compassions fail not. They are new every morning: great is thy faithfulness." (Lamentations 3:22-23)

These verses remind us that God's commitment to us is unwavering, and His mercies are new every morning. He is faithful even when we are not, and His love for us never fails. Considering His great faithfulness, we have every reason to give thanks for the struggles, challenges, blessings, ups and downs, and highs and lows of life. Because God is committed to us, we must be committed to Him. Every new day is an opportunity to renew our commitment and dedicate ourselves to His purposes.

As Maya Angelou wisely said, "If you're trying to be normal, you will never know how amazing you can be." We have a choice: we can settle for a life of mediocrity and commit to being average, or we can strive for greatness and commit to being all that God has called us to be. When we choose the latter, we open ourselves up to a world of possibilities and the chance to make a real difference in the world around us.

Show Up

I've always admired people who are true to their word, do what they say they'll do, show up when they say they'll be there, and follow through on their commitments. These people demonstrate integrity and reliability, and their word carries weight because others know they can be trusted. In a day and age like today, finding committed people is proving to be more challenging than ever. Many people seem to have lost sight of the importance of keeping their word and following through on their commitments. They say one thing and do another or make promises they have no intention of keeping. Some even go so far as to deceive others for no apparent reason, leaving a trail of broken trust and disappointed expectations in their wake.

When you show support for someone, but they fail to reciprocate when you need them, it can be deeply hurtful and discouraging. People may make excuses for why they couldn't keep their word, but at the end of the day, what matters is that they didn't follow through. Even if they don't say anything, their actions (or lack thereof) speak volumes about their level of commitment and reliability. There was a time when a person's word was their bond, and a handshake was as good as a signed contract. Sadly, those days seem to be fading into the past, and genuine commitment is becoming increasingly rare.

But as believers, we are called to a higher standard. Our commitment to God should be the driving force behind everything we do and reflected in how we interact with others. When we make a promise, we should move Heaven and Earth to keep it, even if it means sacrificing comfort or convenience. We should be known as people of integrity whose word can be trusted and whose commitment is unwavering.

Essential Qualities

Commitment is a powerful word that encompasses a wide range of qualities essential for success in any endeavor, whether in our personal lives, relationships, or spiritual journeys. When we break down the concept of commitment, we find that it is built upon a foundation of dedication, loyalty, wholehearted devotion, pledge, priority, sacrifice, and vow.

Dedication is the unwavering focus and determination to see things through, even in the face of challenges or setbacks. It is the willingness to pour our time, energy, and resources into the things that matter most to us without allowing distractions or obstacles to derail us from our purpose. Loyalty is the steadfast allegiance and faithfulness we demonstrate to the people, principles, and beliefs we hold dear. It is the refusal to abandon or betray our commitments, even when remaining true may be difficult or costly.

Wholehearted devotion is the complete and total investment of ourselves into the things we are committed to. It is the willingness to give our all, to hold nothing back, and to approach our commitments with passion, enthusiasm, and sincerity. A pledge is a solemn promise or agreement to follow through on our commitments. It is giving our word and binding ourselves to a course of action, regardless of the challenges or temptations that may arise along the way.

Priority is the recognition that our commitments deserve our highest attention and focus. It is the willingness to put our commitments first, even when other demands or desires compete for our time and energy.

Sacrifice is the understanding that genuine commitment often requires giving up something of value to remain faithful to our pledges. It is the willingness to let go of short-term pleasures, comforts, or conveniences to achieve the long-term goals and rewards that come with keeping our commitments.

Finally, a vow is the most sacred and binding form of commitment. It is the solemn promise we make before God and others to remain steadfast in our devotion, loyalty, and dedication, no matter what challenges or trials we face.

When we cultivate these qualities of commitment in our lives, we position ourselves for success in every area. We become people of integrity whose word can be trusted and whose actions align with our values and beliefs. We develop the resilience and perseverance needed to overcome obstacles and setbacks, knowing that our commitment to the goal is greater than any temporary hardship we may face.

In our walk with God, commitment is essential for growing in faith, character, and intimacy with Him. As we dedicate ourselves wholeheartedly to seeking His will, obeying His Word, and serving His purposes, we experience the joy and fulfillment of fully surrendering to Him. While the journey of commitment is not always easy, it is always worth it. As we remain loyal to our pledges, prioritize our values, and willingly sacrifice for the sake of our convictions, we become people of substance and impact, leaving a legacy of faithfulness and integrity that will inspire others for generations to come.

So, let us embrace the call to commitment in all its facets and expressions. Let us be people of dedication, loyalty, wholehearted devotion, pledge, priority, sacrifice, and vow, knowing that as we do, we will experience the richness and abundance of a life well-lived and a faith that moves mountains.

Commit to God first! No excuses! No distractions! Nothing should ever come between you and your commitment to God: absolutely nothing and no one. When you commit to God, you can be the original, authentic, bold, daring, courageous, and committed person He created you to be. You don't have to conform to the world's standards or try to fit into someone else's mold. You can stand tall in your uniqueness and use your gifts and talents to glorify Him in everything you do.

The Power of Choice

Here is a rhetorical question that continues to trouble my spirit. Why would a perfect God create an ideal world, a perfect garden, a perfect man and woman, and place them in this ideal situation, only to allow them to encounter the grandmaster tempter and be tested by him? Couldn't God, who is omniscient, have foreseen that Satan would be a problem? So why not send this grand tempter to Mars, Venus, Saturn, or Pluto? God could have destroyed him when he revolted in Heaven. Why send him to Earth, into the beautiful garden He created?

The answer lies in the power of choice. God gave Adam and Eve the freedom to choose whom they would serve, and He gives us that same freedom today. They could have easily chosen to stay committed to what God had told them: to eat from every tree except the Tree of the Knowledge of Good and Evil. God gave them everything they needed for a blessed and abundant life, but the tempter caused them to focus on the one thing they did not have. And therein lies the danger. When we lose focus on what we have and place our attention on what we think we need, we risk losing everything.

There's an old saying that a bird in the hand is better than two in the bush. In other words, it's better to be content with what you have than to risk losing it by chasing after something more. When we are grateful for the blessings God has given us and stay committed to the assignment He has placed before us, we position ourselves to receive even more incredible blessings in the future. But when we allow ourselves to be distracted by the allure of the forbidden, we open the door for the enemy to come in and steal, kill, and destroy.

Your Commitment Speaks

Commitment is personal! Commitment is work! Commitment is intentional! It takes sacrifice to be committed!

> ### Your commitment speaks for you.
> ### No one can co-sign for you.

> *"Now when he was in Jerusalem at the passover, in the feast day, many believed in his name, when they saw the miracles which he did. But Jesus did not commit himself unto them, because he knew all men, and needed not that any should testify of man: for he knew what was in man." (John 2:23-25)*

This passage reveals an important truth about commitment. Many people followed Jesus because they were impressed by the miracles He performed, but He did not commit Himself to them because He knew their hearts. He knew their commitment was superficial and self-serving, and He could not entrust Himself to people who were only in it for what they could get out of it.

The same is true for us today. We can fool some people sometimes, but we can never fool Jesus. He sees beyond our outward actions and knows the true motives of our hearts. He cannot commit to uncommitted people because He knows they will eventually fall away when the going gets tough, or they don't get what they want.

If we want to experience the fullness of God's blessings and provision in our lives, we must remain committed to Him no matter what. We can't be fair-weather followers only in it for the good times. We must be willing to stand firm in our faith even when the storms of life are raging all around us. When we commit to God, we can boldly say, "I can do all things through Christ who strengthens me" (Philippians 4:13). However, this commitment requires taking things to the next level.

Commitment Requires Persistence

> *"Wherefore seeing we also are compassed about with so great a cloud of witnesses, let us lay aside every weight, and the sin which doth so easily beset us, and let us run with patience the race that is set before us, Looking unto Jesus the author and finisher of our faith." (Hebrews 12:1-2)*

These verses paint a powerful picture of what next-level commitment looks like. We are surrounded by a great cloud of witnesses who have gone before us, men and women of faith who have finished the race and received their reward. Their testimonies remind us that we, too, must keep going and not give up.

But to run the race with endurance, we must lay aside every weight and sin that so easily entangles us. These things slow us down and hold us back, as do the distractions and temptations that try to pull us off course. We must intentionally identify these things and ruthlessly eliminate them to run unhindered toward the goal.

This is the sin that you never resist, the one you don't ever fight against. Maybe it's a secret addiction or a besetting sin that you've grown comfortable with over time. Whatever it is, it has no place in the life of a fully committed follower of Christ. We must be willing to lay it aside and leave it behind, no matter how difficult or painful.

We must run patiently, remembering that the Christian life is not a sprint but a marathon. We need to pace ourselves and keep our eyes on the finish line, trusting that God will give us the strength and endurance to keep going. This is the essence of next-level commitment: staying committed to your commitment and taking it to the next level.

How Badly Do You Want It?

Next-level commitment requires hunger. How badly do you want it? So what if you are in last place? Stay committed. Many may have been called before you, but you were built for the next level. Finding people like you who will serve the Lord, even in difficult times is hard. People today want to be served, not to serve. It's better to be a giver than a receiver.

Many people today don't want to remain committed when trouble arises. Many have cut and run at the first sign of trouble: a bad marriage—end it, trouble in ministry—find a new one, issues on the job— quit. The list goes on and on. We want to reign without suffering. We want joy without pain, sunshine without rain. We want blessings without suffering. We want rewards without sacrifice. We want our prayers answered without praying. We want God to move quickly while we continue to move slowly. We get in the prayer line on Sunday and want a miracle by Monday. We want the pastor to fast while we have a six-course breakfast (coffee, juice, bacon, toast, eggs, grits, and ham).

But the truth is, you don't deserve what you don't commit to. You can't expect to reap the rewards if you're unwilling to work and make the sacrifices necessary to achieve your goals. God is not a genie in a bottle who exists to grant our every wish without any effort on our part. He is looking for people willing to partner with Him, roll up their sleeves, and do the hard work of building His kingdom.

What Is Next-Level?

- Surpassing your current level
- Advancing to new heights
- Improving in every aspect
- Elevating your game to the next dimension
- Going higher while moving forward and upward

Most people take the elevator to the next level. They want the easy way out, the shortcut to success. But the truth is, there are no shortcuts in the kingdom of God. We must be willing to take the stairs and build endurance and strength by mastering the level we're on before moving on to the next. We must press toward the mark of the prize of the higher calling in God, not settle for a lower level of living.

Some would rather live on the lower level and have the next level with titles and positions handed to them. But have you conquered your lions and bears on this level? Have you stayed overnight in the lion's den of trouble and fear without cursing God? How did you handle your fiery trials in the furnace? Until you have faced and overcome the challenges of your current level, you won't be ready for the more significant challenges that await you on the next level.

Higher levels mean bigger challenges!

Achieving significant goals in life requires a next-level attitude of commitment at the next level. We know what commitment is, but let's consider some requirements: faith to believe it will work, discipline, concentration, self-determination, sacrifice, taking the longer route, and taking the stairs of fasting and praying.

Next-level commitment positions you for purpose. It helps you find God's plan for your life and pursue it with everything you've got. When you are fully committed to His will, He will provide all the provisions you need to see it through. It takes commitment to stay in position, and it takes commitment to finish the course.

We're all committed to something! Unfortunately, most folks are committed to the wrong things. Being lazy, backbiting, and not keeping their word. They are truth-breakers, busybodies, procrastinators, and the list goes on and on. I have never seen such a day when people are undisciplined and unfocused. All because under the pressures of life, they take their eyes off their God-given purpose.

Next-level commitment moves Jesus, inspires people, glorifies God, and horrifies the enemy. It can demolish the spirit of procrastination and prevent the devil from stealing, killing, and destroying your future. He may delay you, but he can't stop you. Next-level commitment is a divine ability that connects you to a God-given purpose, to see it through from beginning to end.

> *"Though he slay me, yet will I trust in him...All the days of my appointed time will I wait, till my change comes."*
> *(Job 13:15, 14:14)*

Next-level commitment carries out God's plan despite the demonic forces opposing the assignment. It continues despite the weapons formed against you.

"Beloved, think it not strange concerning the fiery trial which is to try you, as though some strange thing happened unto you: But rejoice, inasmuch as ye are partakers of Christ's sufferings."
(1 Peter 4:12-13)

"No weapon that is formed against thee shall prosper; and every tongue that shall rise against thee in judgment thou shalt condemn." (Isaiah 54:17)

Your divine assignment continues until the desired results of the designed plan are reached. Must Jesus bear the cross alone, and all the world go free? No, there's a cross for everyone, and there's a cross for me! Earthly thoughts of carnality will attack a heavenly assignment on every side. But a heavenly mind will always rise above your fleshly will.

Next-level commitment focuses on accomplishing the task of a godly assignment despite setbacks, challenges, or obstacles. It refuses to take no for an answer, pushes through the crowds, and sees the desired end, not allowing the issues of life to stop you. Next-level commitment is not concerned with what others say or think as you push through the crowd of pessimists, naysayers, and dream killers. It moves you to accomplish your goals, no matter what.

If we remain committed to what we've committed to God, our heavenly FICO SCORES will continue to increase day after day. Then Jesus will commit to us, as He sees we are not only in it for what we can get from Him. Remember, He knows what's in all of us and needs no one to co-sign for us (John 2:24-25).

So let us take our commitment to the next level, laying aside every weight and sin that so easily besets us and running with patience the race that is set before us. Let us fix our eyes on Jesus, the Author, and Finisher of our faith, and trust Him to lead us into the good works He has prepared for us to walk in. As we remain steadfast in our devotion to Him, we will see our heavenly FICO SCORES soar and experience the fullness of His blessings and favor in every area of our lives.

CHAPTER 4

Obedience Is the Key

Obedience is compliance with what is required of you. Obedience requires submission and must be practiced. Obedience in action is doing what you would not do unless someone in authority or influence told you to do it. To obey is a verb, the action for obedience. To be obedient is an adjective that describes the action of obeying. Obedience is a noun that identifies the condition of being obedient.

In the Old Testament, obedience is to hear, listen, and carry out what is required, to adhere. It carries with it the ethical significance of hearing with reverence to honor and serve, dealing with one's conduct and morals. It was a covenant relationship between God and the Israelites. If they were obedient, then God would bless, provide, and protect.

In the New Testament, obedience is "I hear, so I will obey."

> *"He that hath an ear, let him hear what the Spirit saith unto the churches." (Revelation 3:22)*

Let him obey what the Spirit is saying. We follow Jesus' teachings by making disciples of men, baptizing, healing, feeding the hungry, visiting the fatherless and widows in their affliction, and ministering to those in prison. We must walk as Christ walked, living as He lived—loving and caring for the less fortunate, seeking the lost sheep, and keeping our reputations unspotted from the world.

Satan is the antithesis of obedience, the epitome of disobedience. His one act of civil anti-obedience in Heaven caused him and one-third of the angels in Heaven to be cast out and forfeit all of Heaven's eternal beauty and glory. They only gained the whole world along with eternal damnation.

> *"For what is a man profited, if he shall gain the whole world, and lose his own soul? Or what shall a man give in exchange for his soul?" (Matthew 16:26)*

The soul is the most valuable real estate a person will ever possess. We are all born with bodies, souls, and spirits. Everyone born will die. Man can kill or destroy the body but not the soul (Matthew 10:28). Only you can forfeit your soul, your intellect, by seeking material things such as buildings, land, homes, money, investments, automobiles, etc., which can all be replaced if lost, but not the soul.

> *"For we brought nothing into this world, and it is certain we can carry nothing out." (1 Timothy 6:7)*

When a person dies, the soul and spirit return to God. But the anti-obedient soul shall spend eternity in damnation (Galatians 6:8). Hebrews 4:12 tells us that the Word of God is sharp and powerful enough to separate the soul from the spirit. The spirit will return to God (Ecclesiastes 12:7), but the disobedient soul shall die (Ezekiel 18:4, 20) and be judged based on what we put first in our lives. The paycheck for sin/disobedience is death (Romans 6:23). Disobedience costs way too much!

Spirit and Truth

Our spirits are where we connect with and worship God in spirit and truth (John 4:24)—a connection of obedience, trust, love, dependency, and worship. It's where our faith is activated as our spirits connect with His Spirit. It's what directs us to seek first the kingdom of God and His righteousness (Matthew 6:33), trusting the scriptures that the kingdom of God is not about meat, drink, or material things. Instead, it's where we understand that the kingdom of God is righteousness, joy, and peace in the Holy Spirit (Romans 14:17). When we pause for praise instead of succumbing to sin, Satan seizes the opportunity. Knowing his time is short, he prowls the earth seeking to deceive and overthrow with lies and deceitful words.

Satan presented the very first man and woman, Adam and Eve, with the only thing he could—a lie. Before this encounter, Adam and Eve only knew and heard truth, as they always heard the voice of God strolling through the garden calling them in the cool of the day. Shame quickly set in as the realization of their nakedness caused them to hide for fear of the truth of their disobedience. Acting upon Satan's deceit caused disobedience/sin/unrighteousness to be born into the earthly realm, which was not the will of God. His will being done in Heaven is what He desired for Earth. But because of disobedience, we now pray, "Thy will be done in earth, as it is in heaven." (Matthew 6:10)

The first time a lie was heard, believed, and acted upon, it cost Adam and Eve the Garden of Eden. In turn, this brought a curse into the world: enmity between Satan, the woman, and their descendants; labor pains in childbearing; and hard, manual, sweat-from-the-brow labor for man. That one act of disobedience resulted in everyone after them being born into sin and shaped in iniquity. Obedience meant they were free to eat from every tree except the Tree of the Knowledge of Good and Evil. If the deceiver cared about them, why didn't he tell them to first eat from the

Tree of Life to live forever? Then, they could have eaten from the Tree of the Knowledge of Good and Evil. This suggests that Satan does not want anyone to outlive him.

Satan plans to lure anyone who will listen and believe the big lie, causing us to deny the truth and walk in disobedience. Satan is exceptionally good at his job. He deceived one-third of the angels in Heaven who knew God, worshipped God, and lived with God. He convinced these angels to leave Heaven and follow him. He fooled Eve, the first woman, and her husband, Adam. He also fooled Samson, the strongest man, and King Solomon, the wisest man.

He is an anointed cherub, a masterful angelic musician from Heaven, created with beauty and adorned with precious stones, gold, and musical pipes. His anointed musical gifts are far superior to anything anyone has ever heard. Known as the morning star, his beauty is more alluring, enticing, and deceptive than anything our eyes have ever seen. He uses the three elements embedded in our DNA to lure us: the lust of our flesh, the lust of our eyes, and the pride of life. He has nothing new to offer, just a remix that plays on our lustful flesh, lust-filled eyes, and prideful life. It is the same old song in a repackaged container. This skillful chief musician, cast out of Heaven, knows exactly what key to play to make us lose focus and walk in disobedience. Walking in obedience or disobedience is intentional. Let us not live by accident but intentionally in everything we do.

Have you heard of the Pied Piper of Hamelin? A figure in German folklore, the legend of the Pied Piper dates back to the Middle Ages. The earliest references describe a piper, dressed in multicolored clothing, who was a rat-catcher hired by a town to lure rats away with his magical pipes. When the town refused to pay for his services rendered, he used his instrument's magical power on their children, leading them away just as he had led the rats. Satan was much like the Pied Piper but more deadly. Satan uses his power of influence to lead us away from the presence of God.

"Let no man say when he is tempted, I am tempted of God: for God cannot be tempted with evil, neither tempteth he any man: But every man is tempted, when he is drawn away of his own lust, and enticed." (James 1:13-14)

The Cost of Disobedience

When we allow our lusts and the allure of what we see and hear to drive us, the two fornicate together and conceive a child called sin. When we allow sin to fully develop, it brings death. Temptation arises from our lust and the allure of what we see and hear, which, if followed, will lead to the disobedience that results in death. The cost of disobedience is too high, leading us to lose everything.

Disobedience cost Moses the promised land. Disobedience cost King Saul his kingdom. Disobedience cost me more than eight years of struggling with crack cocaine addiction. It cost me family, friends, reputation, health, finances, etc. Imagine if we were obedient to the Word of God, it would save us a lifetime of heartaches, headaches, loss, confusion, and drama. Deuteronomy 28:1-14 speaks of blessings in exchange for obedience, while the remaining verses foretell curses for disobedience. Although this Old Testament passage is specifically addressed to the children of Israel, the principle of obedience or disobedience, blessings or curses, applies to everyone. Whether you obey or disobey, you will receive blessings or curses. Some call it karma; I call it the law of reciprocity.

Jesus Christ is the only person born who never deviated from obedience. A good friend of mine, Keith J. Williams, Pastor of New Beginnings Church in Oakland, CA, made a profound statement: "Jesus was born with the cross in sight, ready to die." This tells me that He looked beyond the cross to you and me in complete obedience to the Father's will. He had plenty of opportunities and hardships to quit, give up, and say, "This is way too much. I can't do it."

"Let this mind be in you, which was also in Christ Jesus: Who, being in the form of God, thought it not robbery to be equal with God: But made himself of no reputation, and took upon him the form of a servant, and was made in the likeness of men: And being found in fashion as a man, he humbled himself, and became obedient unto death, even the death of the cross. Wherefore God also hath highly exalted him, and given him a name which is above every name." (Philippians 2:5-9)

Savior, Rescuer, Healer, Deliverer

Jesus is the Author and Finisher of our faith, the Alpha and Omega. He is the road map for how to live a complete life of obedience to God. How did Jesus do it? Can we agree it would have been unrealistic for Jesus to use His divine abilities to complete His assignment, then ask you and me to go through, hold on, not give up, turn the other cheek, love your enemies, hold your peace, or bear your cross without using divine ability, which we do not possess as human beings? For this reason and this reason alone, Jesus could not use His heavenly powers to carry out His earthly assignment.

So how did He do it? By getting away from the noise of His boys and going to a secluded place. He spent time alone with God, fasted, prayed, and talked to God all night. Rising early, He prepared for His ministry. By living a life of prayer, not a prayer life but a life of prayer, He was always connected to God and ready to do His will. We also must escape the noise of social media and hanging out with our friends to be prepared to do His will. We need to develop a life of prayer and obedience to the will of God if we want our heavenly FICO SCORES to increase. Learn to go through and hold on during disappointments, when we're mistreated, misunderstood, lied on, in distress, lonely, heartbroken, and depressed about our circumstances. Jesus will never leave or forsake us. But the originator of lies will tell you Jesus does not care about you. This is not true. He is there, ready to help us in times of trouble. Through Him, we can do all things.

My friends, we must practice becoming intentional in everything we do: work, play, praise and worship, fasting, eating, exercise, relaxing, praying, and forgiving. Being obedient is intentional, just as disobedience is intentional and no accident. If we intentionally obey God's Word, we will see our heavenly FICO SCORES increase. When walking in the disobedience of sin, it's either by omission or commission, intentionally or unintentionally. When we omit to do the right thing, it is called the sin of omission (James 4:17). The other way we sin is by commission. This can be intentional or unintentional, knowingly or unknowingly doing wrong or taking something.

"For all have sinned, and come short of the glory of God."
(Romans 3:23)

Thank God for His grace that forgives, heals, restores, empowers, and encourages us to raise our heavenly FICO SCORES despite falling short of righteousness.

"But he giveth more grace. Wherefore he saith, God resisteth the proud, but giveth grace unto the humble. Submit yourselves therefore to God. Resist the devil, and he will flee from you."
(James 4:6-7)

Grace and favor are given to the humble and obedient, but God resists the proud and disobedient. If we submit to God and resist the devil, he will flee from us. Most people have it backward. They obey the desires of their flesh and resist God and truth.

> **Obedience requires a willingness
> to submit to God.**

We submit to God because He is our Creator, our everything. Without God, we are nothing. By submitting to Him, we can do all things through Christ who strengthens us (Philippians 4:13). Obedience is not weakness because we submit; it's the opposite. It is a form of self-control, a quiet strength. We expect obedience from our children and our pets. If we adhere to the rules set by God, we can raise our heavenly FICO SCORES.

If we follow the rules set by credit bureaus, paying our bills on time, perhaps setting up automatic payments, and keeping our credit usage below one-third while preventing any future negative items, our credit scores will gradually improve. However, it will take effort on your part: sacrifice, obedience, patience, discipline, and persistence—just as you would do when seeking the kingdom of God and His righteousness (Matthew 6:33).

CHAPTER 5

Sanctification
Is a Process

Sanctification, the process of being set apart for God's purposes and growing in holiness, is a critical component of our spiritual journey. It's not a one-time event but a lifelong process that requires dedication, perseverance, and a deep reliance on God's grace. In this chapter, we will delve into the concept of sanctification and explore how it relates to our heavenly FICO SCORES. We will look at the role of the Holy Spirit in our sanctification, the importance of daily surrender, and the transformative power of God's Word. As we embrace the process of sanctification, we will discover that it not only brings us closer to God but also empowers us to live a life that is pleasing to Him.

The word "sanctify" in the Greek means "to set apart." The word "sanctification" refers to the process of "setting apart," which comes from the Greek word *hagiasmos*—to consecrate for the purpose of making something holy. "Holy" and "sanctify" are synonymous with being set apart. Being holy is the action of being sanctified.

> *"I beseech you therefore, brethren, by the mercies of God, that ye present your bodies a living sacrifice, holy, acceptable unto God, which is your reasonable service." (Romans 12:1)*

When I was growing up, birthdays and Christmas were always special, even for us, despite not having much. We looked forward to receiving just one or two presents. And it was unheard of to give a person a present without first gift wrapping it. The suspense of the gift wrap added to the excitement of opening it. Presentation is everything, and by wrapping the present, the recipient would not know the contents until it was opened. Our bodies are the gifts we submit to God and must be wrapped in holiness, which is acceptable and our reasonable obligation. So, when God sees us, the gifts, He sees the time we took to present our lives in His image and likeness of sanctification, which is for His good pleasure. Our bodies, souls, and spirits belong to God, and we must set them apart. It is the least we can do for the One who has done so much for us. To truly raise our heavenly FICO SCORES, we must work on sanctifying ourselves. Sanctification will definitely boost your heavenly SCORES in no time. Try it! Then and only then can we come boldly to the throne of grace.

> *"Let us therefore come boldly unto the throne of grace, that we*
> *may obtain mercy, and find grace to help in time of need."*
> *(Hebrews 4:16)*

Trust the Process

Sanctification is a process. You may have tried and failed but keep at it. In fact, sanctification is a lifetime process of continuous growth.

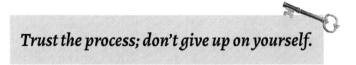

Trust the process; don't give up on yourself.

When I first began my journey of sanctification, I struggled with letting go of my old habits and thought patterns. But as I spent more time in prayer and meditation on God's Word, I began to experience a deeper level of cleansing and renewal. The process wasn't always easy, but it was necessary for my spiritual growth.

Since January 17, 1992, I've been perfecting my process of serving God. First and foremost, I learned to keep my eyes straight ahead, focusing on my own journey of salvation without comparing myself to others. Let me be real with you—I did not accept Christ at an early age. I struggled through years of bumping my head, trying to navigate life's challenges. After hitting rock bottom—sick and tired of the drugs, sex, alcohol, parties, and eight years of giving my money to drug dealers—I finally surrendered my life to Christ.

You see, I grew up in a strict, sanctified home raised by a single mother. We were not allowed to listen to secular music, attend parties, drink, smoke, or gamble. Church taught us the importance of living authentically before God and warned against hypocrisy. Salvation meant no participation in anything that might compromise our faith. Growing up, I was passionate about sports—running, jumping, climbing, playing baseball, and tackle football. Despite my small size—never weighing more than 147 pounds—I was the fastest kid in my neighborhood. By the time I reached sophomore year through senior year, I had become one of the fastest students in my high school. I loved playing baseball, football, and running track. Mom only let me play organized baseball because it was free at Grant Elementary in Richmond. I dreamed of playing football, but we couldn't afford organized sports.

By the time I got to high school, I had played hundreds of hours of tackle football at the neighborhood park. However, getting tackled with pads was completely different, and in my first high school freshman game, I fumbled five times. I wonder if I had played in the Pop Warner youth football league as a youngster, how things would have turned out. Parents, please allow your children to play organized sports. It gives them the advantage of learning the fundamentals and does not allow them to quit just because it's hard. To this day, I wonder how good I really could have been if I had started earlier. In the next game, I had a breakout performance, outrunning the defense for a 19-yard touchdown run and zero fumbles. Frustrated with the demanding practices and coaches yelling at me, I quit the team. Consequently, the following year, I was not allowed to play because of my decision to quit the previous season. Being raised by a single mother and attending a holiness church, sports were frowned upon.

Calling My Name

To be fully transparent, staying focused and disciplined in following Christ after experiencing deliverance and being filled with the Holy Ghost required immense effort. Satan frequently attacked me in my sleep with dreams of drugs and wild parties. The battle against addictions— drugs, alcohol, nicotine, and sex—was constant, with crack cocaine being a significant challenge during my first four years walking with God.

My support system was invaluable; without it, I would not have persevered. This support came from many strong individuals, including Pastor James and the late Marjorie Taylor of West Contra Costa Christian Center in Richmond, CA. Pastor Marjorie inspired me to pursue a real estate license, and their church community, which operated as a 24/7 ministry, provided crucial support.

Although I grew up in a sanctified home and attended a sanctified church, it was not open around the clock. I am deeply grateful to the saints at Faith Temple COGIC, particularly the late Pastor Archie Brice and Lady Josephine Brice. My late mother, Eliza Featherstone, prayed faithfully for me as I struggled with addiction.

My cousin, Elder (now Pastor) Albert Featherstone, played a pivotal role in my journey. His dedication to sanctified living challenged my misconceptions about Christianity being merely a crutch for the elderly. Witnessing his transformation convinced me that Jesus could change my life as well. Evangelist Gloria Dean Howard and my mother spent years praying for me while I wandered the streets of Richmond. Our late Church Mother, Gaynell Lewis, and Deacon Edward (Pops) Lewis welcomed my wife, Prophetess Shirley McCord-Featherstone, and me into their home countless times. They guided us through discussions on faith, marriage, ministry, and love. We attended Holy Convocations, Women's Conventions, AIMS Conventions, and Leadership Conferences of the Church of God in Christ, where their encouragement sustained us.

My lovely wife was the most influential person who believed in me and married me just one year after my salvation. Her unwavering trust, love, encouragement, and prayers kept me grounded on the right path. Whenever I faced challenging real estate deals, I leaned on Shirley's prayers, and she always assured me, "It's already done because you have favor with God. He will take care of you to take care of me."

My support network is extensive, and I'm forever grateful to everyone who has shaped who I am today. Their prayers, encouragement, and God's grace and mercy have carried me far. Sanctification is not a quick fix—it's a journey filled with challenges, frustrations, and messy moments. Sometimes, you may feel alone in your struggles, but remember, Jesus promised to never leave us or forsake us.

It's a Journey

The process of sanctification is a journey; the acronym for JOURNEY is Just Open Up, Right's Never Easy, Yield! I rely on my support system, the people who prayed and guided me toward my destiny. Only you know where you are in the process of submitting yourself to be holy for God and His purpose.

So where do we begin? With confession! Confess that we are sinners in need of a Savior. Confess sins of unrighteousness and repent, renouncing our sinful lifestyles, which means doing a 180-degree turn. In Chapter 4, I discussed the sins of omission and commission. Sin, in simple terms, means falling short of a mark or standard. Sanctification is a standard. A holy God will not lower His standard for anyone. The standard is righteousness, to be just. So, all unrighteousness is sin. To be unjust is to be unholy.

If we ever hope to improve our heavenly FICO SCORES, we must confess that Jesus Christ has come into our lives, that He was crucified; He bled and died on a cross, was buried, and rose three days later with the power to save, heal, deliver, rescue, bless, protect, cover, and sustain us. Then, we are rescued/saved! Then, the process of becoming sanctified begins. It is the process of separating from our old selves, ways, thoughts, habits, and actions. Places we used to go, we don't go back to. Things we used to do, we have to give up. People we used to associate with, we let go of. Sanctification is the process of removing the old so we can walk into the new.

> *"Therefore if any man be in Christ, he is a new creature: old things are passed away; behold, all things are become new."*
> *(2 Corinthians 5:17)*

The process of transformation takes place, and we learn a new way of living. The acronym for TRUST is Totally Rely Upon the Savior's Thoughts. To do this, we have to get sick and tired of being sick and tired of our old selves that continue to get us in over our heads. Only then can real transformation begin, but we have to want to change.

He gave us free will. This is strictly voluntary, or the change will not last.

> **No one can force change on anyone else, not even God.**

Being Filled

The next level of sanctification is receiving and being filled with the Holy Ghost, which is freely given to anyone who asks for it. It's simple. After you have repented of your sins and asked Jesus to come into your heart, open your mind to receive the Holy Ghost. Your mind must be free from all distracting thoughts that can and will come up while you're in the process of receiving. Then, we can ask the Father, in Jesus' name, to fill us with the Holy Ghost.

Pause. Ready? Try this now:

1. Clear your mind and ask God, in Jesus' name, to forgive you of all sins.

2. Believe in your heart that you are forgiven and saved.

3. Confess that you are saved!

4. Say, "Fill me, Jesus, with the Holy Ghost. Fill me, Jesus. Fill me, Jesus. Fill me, Jesus."

5. Continue to ask Jesus to fill you with the Holy Ghost. Repeat this over and over with a clear mind. "Fill me, Jesus."

Did He fill you? Did you receive it? Did you speak with new tongues?

This is how I received the Holy Ghost, also known as the Holy Spirit, and began to speak in a new language to God (speaking in unknown tongues), my heavenly Father. I had to keep my thoughts free from everything, except being filled with the Holy Spirit, and I was. When I received the Holy Ghost, I started speaking in unknown tongues and knew I was filled with His Spirit. Some believe and teach that you don't receive the Holy Spirit unless you have evidence of speaking in other tongues. Others teach that you don't need to speak in other tongues to be filled with the Holy Spirit. Here's what I'm saying: when I was filled, I did speak in an unknown tongue.

My goal here is not to convince, force, or criticize anyone who has not spoken in other tongues upon receiving the Holy Ghost. So, let's examine the Scriptures regarding receiving the Holy Ghost and the purpose of tongues.

On the day of Pentecost, the disciples and others were in one place, at one time, in one agreement.

> *"And they were all filled with the Holy Ghost, and began to speak with other tongues, as the Spirit gave them utterance." (Acts 2:4)*

The purpose was not to edify themselves as I did when I was filled with the Holy Ghost.

> *"And there were dwelling at Jerusalem Jews, devout men, out of every nation under heaven. Now when this was noised abroad, the multitude came together, and were confounded, because that every man heard them speak in his own language." (Acts 2:5-6)*

So, the purpose of tongues when the disciples received the Holy Ghost on the day of Pentecost was twofold.

1. To give the recipients power to be witnesses everywhere and all the time.
2. To bring the languages back together to reverse the curse found in Genesis 11:1, 4, 6-7, 9—the Tower of Babel.

Vs. 1: "And the whole earth was of one language, and of one speech."

Vs. 4: "And they said, Go to, let us build us a city and a tower, whose top may reach unto heaven; and let us make us a name, lest we be scattered abroad upon the face of the whole earth."

Vs. 6: "And the LORD said, Behold, the people is one, and they have all one language; and this they begin to do: and now nothing will be restrained from them, which they have imagined to do."

That statement reminds me of 1 Corinthians 1:10: "Now I beseech you, brethren, by the name of our Lord Jesus Christ, that ye all speak the same thing, and that there be no divisions among you; but that ye be perfectly joined together in the same mind and in the same judgment."

Vs. 7: Speaking to the Holy Ghost, the Lord says, "Go to, let us go down, and there confound their language, that they may not understand one another's speech."

Vs. 9: "Therefore is the name of it called Babel; because the LORD did there confound the language of all the earth: and from thence did the LORD scatter them abroad upon the face of all the earth."

Back to the Day of Pentecost, they were in one place, with the same mind, in one agreement. Then suddenly, a sound from Heaven came as a rushing mighty wind, which filled everyone with the Holy Ghost. They began to speak in different languages, confounding the city, as every man heard them speaking in their own language. This was not the tongues that edified the speaker but the person hearing.

In Acts 10:45-46, the gift of the Holy Spirit was first given to the Gentiles, and they began to speak with tongues at Cornelius' house. 1 Corinthians 12:10 speaks of different kinds of tongues and interpretation of tongues. Continuing to verse 30, "Do all speak with tongues?" Then 1 Corinthians 14:2 says, "He that speaks in an unknown tongue speaks not unto men, but unto God." Verse 4 says, "He that speaks in an unknown tongue edifies himself." However, prophecy edifies the hearer. Apostle Paul says in the next verse, "I would that ye spake with tongues, but rather that ye prophesied" (1 Corinthians 14:5).

When I received the gift of the Holy Spirit, I spoke in an unknown tongue to God. In that moment, it was better than any feeling I have ever experienced: self-gratification, sex, drugs, alcohol, satisfying my sweet tooth, better than any meal you could imagine. It was simply the best feeling ever, all rolled into one. I have never experienced anything like the feeling received from communicating in my heavenly language to God.

Can a person receive the Holy Spirit without speaking in an unknown tongue? What does the Bible say about this?

Over the years, I have seen people who claim to have the Holy Spirit and speak in unknown tongues yet display mean, bitter, angry, and hateful behavior. Galatians 5:22-23 states, "But the fruit of the Spirit [Holy Spirit] is love, joy, peace, long-suffering, gentleness, goodness, faith, meekness, temperance: against such there is no law." These are the byproducts of the Spirit of God—not tongues, but fruit—that produce sanctification. Nowhere does the scripture mention tongues; it only speaks of the fruitful Spirit. Cultivating the fruit of the Spirit is essential to living a sanctified life.

This was not the end, just the beginning. The longer you stay in the presence of God, the more He will show you your flaws, and the more you'll need His sanctifying power. Welcome to the journey of raising your heavenly FICO SCORES. The process requires intentional work. We must pay attention to our daily living habits: who, how, and what we spend our time, resources, and energy on.

The Struggle Is Real

In this process, we are learning how to be holy, grow in grace, not lean on the walls of credit, always needing to borrow forgiveness, and intentionally living daily. Knowing what Jesus did on Calvary's cross to pay our sin debt, we should not continue to borrow against His act. The interest rates are too high, the penalty is too much, and sin gets us deeper in debt.

> *"For the wages which sin pays is death, but the [bountiful] free gift of God is eternal life through (in union with) Jesus Christ our Lord." (Romans 6:23 AMPC)*

Many of us struggle to stay sanctified and live holy. As we grow in God and learn why we suffer, we must tell our flesh "No". Remain content and consistent. We must die to the flesh. Many people struggle because they don't want to let go of their sinful appetites. We must totally surrender to the will and plan of God for our lives. Give up the world to gain Christ. Many of us struggle when we are not called to struggle but suffer. We will continue to struggle until we trust Him and surrender our will so His will can be done.

We are struggling to make ends meet only because we spend so much time pretending to be more than we are, buying things on credit we cannot afford, trying to impress people, hoping they believe we are who we are not. That person at the stop sign only saw my car and not me for thirty seconds, but now, I have sixty to eighty-four months to get out of debt. It's time to stop pretending and going deeper into debt and sin and elevate our heavenly FICO SCORES. We won't require a miracle to get us out because we refuse to sanctify ourselves by setting ourselves apart from this world.

> *"Let your conversation be without covetousness; and be content with such things as ye have: for he hath said, I will never leave thee, nor forsake thee." (Hebrews 13:5)*

> *"Love not the world, neither the things that are in the world. If any man love the world, the love of the Father is not in him. For all that is in the world, the lust of the flesh, and the lust of the eyes, and the pride of life, is not of the Father, but is of the world." (1 John 2:15-16)*

Galatians 6:7-9 DRF Version:

Vs. 7: "Be not deceived; God cannot be tricked (Our FICO SCORES cannot be outwitted) for whatever a person sows (continually), they will receive. (We decide our harvest, if it is good or bad, by what we continue to plant. What we plant will grow.)"

Vs. 8: "The person that sows to their flesh shall of the flesh reap corruption (unanswered prayers, low FICO SCORES) but the person that sows to the Spirit shall of the Spirit reap life everlasting (prayers answered, higher FICO SCORES, the desires of their hearts)."

Vs. 9: "So then do not be weary in doing well (the right things: praying, fasting, loving even our enemies, paying bills on time, keeping our credit usage below one-third) for in due season we shall receive higher FICO SCORES if we don't stop. There will be a great recompense of reward, with our FICO SCORES skyrocketing greatly over time, eventually maximizing to the highest level possible."

So, let's do what King David did in Psalm 51:10. Ask the Father to "Create in me a clean heart, O God; and renew a right spirit within me."

Even the great Apostle Paul continued to grow as he stated:

> *"Brothers and sisters, I do not consider that I have made it my own yet; but one thing I do: forgetting what lies behind and reaching forward to what lies ahead, I press on toward the goal to win the [heavenly] prize of the upward call of God in Christ Jesus." (Philippians 3:13-14 AMP)*

Now that we've begun practicing sanctification and holiness, it's important to remember that we will make mistakes. Give yourself the grace to keep moving forward. I have been on my sanctification journey for over 32 years, and believe me, it is a process. I've made many mistakes along the way—just ask my wife, Shirley, with whom I've shared over 31 years, or any of our children: Kiani, Donnie Jr., Lavarius, Latoya, Latreese, Paulette, and Paul Jr. Yet, I strive to follow the apostle Paul's example: forgetting the mistakes of my past and pushing forward toward my future in God. Forgetting does not mean I ignore or fail to confess my mistakes, but rather that I refuse to let them imprison me or cause me to adopt a victim mindset. If we can continue to press on despite our past and current circumstances, pursuing God's higher calling and trusting in His purpose for our lives while practicing holiness, our heavenly FICO SCORES will soar to new heights.

So, let's stay focused, dedicated, and persistent. Let's be intentional about strategizing with God through fasting and praying for His purpose and plan to be revealed in our lives. Watch what you do today because you'll have to sit in it tomorrow. You've got this. God's got you. You can do this. Keep Him first. Stay sanctified. Owe no one anything except love. Manage your finances wisely. Minimize your use of credit as much as possible.

Moving forward, let's reject the consumer mindset of excessive spending, shopping until we drop, eating until we're stuffed, and using entertainment to live vicariously watching others win and fulfill their purpose, only to remain frustrated in our struggles. Instead, let's seek God first and His righteousness so we can become the best versions of ourselves. Let's focus on consecrating each day to the Lord and witness our heavenly FICO SCORES increase. How will we know? That's a good question.

> *"If you abide in me, and my words abide in you, you shall ask what you will, and it shall be done unto you." (John 15:7)*

Watch God/Mr. FICO Himself raise your heavenly SCORES.

> *"And may the very God of peace sanctify you completely, and may your whole spirit, soul, and body be preserved blameless at the coming of our Lord Jesus Christ." (1 Thessalonians 5:23)*

CHAPTER 6

The Power of Change

Change! What a mighty and transformative word! Change is about becoming better, different, and newer. It's about replacing old mindsets, altering our game plans, modifying our next steps, and picking up the coins of wisdom and growth.

But why should we change? The answer is simple: to become a better version of ourselves. Change is inevitable, regardless of how we feel about it. Everything in life must change—seasons, circumstances, careers, time, and even people. The following verse represents a season of change.

> *"For we know that if our earthly house of this tabernacle were dissolved, we have a building of God, an house not made with hands, eternal in the heavens." (2 Corinthians 5:1)*

Our earthly bodies are temporary and will eventually dissolve, but we have the assurance of an eternal home with God, not made by human hands. This truth reminds us that change is a natural part of our journey, and we should embrace it as we look forward to our ultimate destination.

It is important to note that Jesus Christ is the only one who does not need to change. As Hebrews 13:8 declares, "Jesus Christ the same yesterday, and today, and forever." He is the constant in our lives, the anchor that holds us steady amid life's storms and transitions.

How Do We Change?

Now, the question arises: How do we change? Changing is one of the most challenging things a person must learn to do to continue growing and achieving different results. Albert Einstein famously said, "Insanity is doing the same thing repeatedly and expecting different results." If we want to see different outcomes in our lives, we must be willing to change our actions and attitudes.

Think about it this way: if we're trying to lose weight, we must eat less frequently and move more. If we're trying to save money, we must spend less than we make. Change is always involved, whether we finish a project or pursue any other goal. We must be willing to alter the direction we're headed in to reach our desired destination.

For me, writing this book required significant change. I had to spend less time with friends on social media and streaming platforms. Instead, I had to start spending more time with my ghostwriter, the Holy Ghost. It was a necessary shift in priorities to accomplish the task.

Change entails becoming different, reinventing oneself, and experiencing a change in form, appearance, and character. It's about being transformed back to the original plan—what God created us to be, not a copy or a duplicate acting like someone else. It's like the old commercial from the 70s and 80s that asked, "Is it live, or is it Memorex?" The company had to change and go through multiple acquisitions to stay relevant. The truth is everything must change. Even the COVID-19 pandemic altered the landscape of how churches, nations, states, and businesses operate.

It's important to recognize that doing something unfamiliar is not always pleasant or easy. It's not always enjoyable. Sometimes, it's painful, scary, confusing, and misunderstood. But if we don't want to remain stagnant, change is essential. The only thing I don't like to change is my barber. He always jokingly asks, "The usual cut?" and I respond, "If it ain't broke, don't fix it. (lol)"

Change Takes Time

A few years ago, my grandson Calvin and I were leaving a grocery store and headed back to the car. I was in a hurry to get to our next destination, I noticed that Calvin was not following me but had stopped and was stooping down. I spoke in a concerned tone, "What are you doing?" He said, "I'm picking up change." I said, "Come on, boy, I got no time for change." He didn't pay me any attention but continued picking up change. So, I waited for him in an impatient demeanor. After he finished, he accumulated a nice piece of change. And I had just told him I had no time for change. This taught me to take time for change and never hinder a person's change process. Allow others to change at their speed; quit being impatient and allow the process to manifest. Remember, we didn't reach our current position overnight—it took time. So, be patient and allow others to enjoy their own process of transformation.

Many rush the process and miss the blessing of transformation. They rush through life, missing moments to smell the roses, pick the flowers, inhale and exhale the fresh air. They miss the movement of life by being trapped in the present moment. They are too impatient to allow the process of disappointment to manifest into positive change.

Changing one's attitude takes time. I remember the lessons my mother gave me and my siblings, my eldest late brother Sammy (God bless his soul), and my younger siblings Rayfus and Dana. I don't remember them getting many smackdowns because we were always good children. When she did get us, she said, "This hurts me more than it will you!" We didn't understand that Mom never wanted to whip us; she always instructed us to do the right thing and change before she would lower the boom. She would wait all day, sometimes two days, until we were in bed and almost asleep, and then we felt the crack of the belt. She wanted us to change and do good. She never got us when she was angry; she never got us for doing good and would never allow us to get away with doing evil, always allowing her rod and staff to instruct, direct, and correct. Thank you, Momma, for your love, protection, direction, and correction. I am forever grateful.

> *"Therefore I urge you, brothers and sisters, by the mercies of God, to present your bodies as a living and holy sacrifice, acceptable to God, which is your spiritual service of worship. And do not be conformed to this world, but be transformed by the renewing of your mind, so that you may prove what the will of God is, that which is good and acceptable and perfect."*
>
> *(Romans 12:1-2 NASB)*

To change, one must transform from their current state to the desired state. One must resist the status quo of habits, practices, peer pressure, rituals, and religion. The Bible says we must be transformed, not conformed to this world's systems. To change, one must shed one's immature self, as we're not truly changing if we keep our old ways and unproductive habits.

We must let go of our old, immature ways of reacting and doing. The old way of life must die to allow the new, transformed life to emerge. Our immature self must be shed for the mature, transformed self to be resurrected. Just as Christ had to die to be resurrected, there are times when our old, immature, and carnal thoughts, mind, and self must die. This is what it means to be transformed: to let the old die so the new can be born, a daily putting off of the old, natural man. Immaturity conforms, maturity transforms.

"Therefore if anyone is in Christ [that is, grafted in, joined to Him by faith in Him as Savior], he is a new creature [reborn and renewed by the Holy Spirit]; the old things [the previous moral and spiritual condition] have passed away. Behold, new things have come [because spiritual awakening brings a new life]." (2 Corinthians 5:17 AMP)

For a caterpillar to change into a butterfly, its organs must undergo change, which is called metamorphosis. Some common synonyms of metamorphose are conversion, transfiguration, and transformation, just to name a few. While all these words mean "to change a thing into a different thing," the process of transformation from an immature state to an adult state involves two or more distinct stages. It is safe to say the caterpillar is immature, and the butterfly is mature.

Inside the cocoon/pupa, the first stage, the caterpillar's body breaks down into a kind of soup and is reorganized into the adult structures of the butterfly. This stage can take 5-21 days and sometimes up to three weeks, waiting for better conditions like rain. Finally, the adult butterfly emerges from the pupa transformed. Adult butterflies will mate, the female will lay eggs, and the life cycle starts over. If we genuinely want to transform, the process does not have to take long; with trial and error, some can change in weeks or even days. If we continue this lifestyle of maturity, we will begin to look at the world, politics, religion, and self differently.

Change prepares us to be restored, so we can partner with others and become ambassadors of transformation. By patiently guiding others through the stages of preparation, healing, and partnership, we help them become witnesses to change.

Action Plan

Centuries ago, Lao Tzu, a philosopher of ancient China, famously quoted, and I paraphrase, "To reach maturity, we must refocus our thoughts, our words, our actions, and our habits. As we are unconsciously forming our character, shaping our destiny."

- We must think on things that add virtue—our thoughts (Phil. 4:8)

- Death and life are in the power of the tongue; we eat what we speak—our words (Prov. 18:21)

- Rejoice in the Lord always, and again I say rejoice—our actions (Phil. 4:4)

- I will bless the Lord at all times, and His praises will always be in my mouth—our habits (Psalm 34:1)

- Set our affection on things above, not on things on the earth—our character (Col. 3:2)

- Eye has not seen, ear has not heard, nor our heart received—our destiny (1 Cor. 2:9)

Many are overdue for change, so they should begin formulating an action plan. Through consistent practices, actions become momentum as we continue to evolve and sharpen our personalities into those in Christ Jesus (Phil. 2:5).

To reach our goals, we must change. We must change or stay in a place of insanity, as Einstein said, "Doing the same thing over and over, expecting a different result." Dealing with life's disasters will slow down your progress, sometimes causing you to drag your feet on Bottleneck Highway, leaving you stuck on Procrastination Drive, heading toward Disappointment Avenue, where you end up parked on Dead End Lane, causing you to feel life is recycling you into a perpetual Groundhog Day.

Life is too short, Heaven is too wonderful, and Hell is too long to continue going in the same direction with no productivity to show for our efforts. It's time to change. God has no respect of persons; He will do for you what He has done for others. So, what gives?

> *"In the year that king Uzziah died, I saw also the Lord sitting upon a throne, high and lifted up, and his train filled the temple." (Isaiah 6:1)*

Never allow anyone to have this much power over you. Isaiah did not change until Uzziah died. His transformation journey didn't occur while he focused on others. Change is different, unfamiliar, and unsettling; change is difficult. People resist change for various reasons: it's new and different. People don't want to lose status, control, power, or security. Some do not think it's necessary; some fear the unknown, and some fear failure—the feeling of being replaced by something new or someone better. Whether to change or not to change is the question. To stay the course could lead to destruction. So, change is inevitable for everyone; we must learn to evolve to excel, or we will only exist. The issue then becomes are we willing to go outside our comfort zone to reach our full potential?

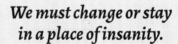

We must change or stay in a place of insanity.

Evolve

One of the most challenging things a person must learn is how to change. To change, one must convert oneself to a new and improved state. One must resist the status quo of habits, practices, peer pressure, and rituals. Change requires maturing from immaturity. When we mature, we become entirely different from what we were before. What use is it to discipline the immature me when it works for a mature me? Immaturity reacts. Maturity responds.

We preach to reach everyone, encouraging people to shift from doing wrong to doing right, to transition from bad to good, to change their actions and habits from spending to saving, and from being liars to truth-tellers.

"Behold, I was shapen in iniquity; and in sin did my mother conceive me." (Psalm 51:5)

We must change. Jesus made it clear in His conversation with Nicodemus:

"Jesus answered and said unto him, Verily, verily, I say unto thee, Except a man be born again, he cannot see the kingdom of God. Nicodemus saith unto him, How can a man be born when he is old? Can he enter the second time into his mother's womb, and be born? Jesus answered, Verily, verily, I say unto thee, Except a man be born of water and of the Spirit, he cannot enter into the kingdom of God." (John 3:3-5)

We can change, improve, and elevate our standards regardless of age. We can transition from mediocrity to excellence, surpassing the average and performing at a higher level.

We want everyone else to change but ourselves. However, we must be the first partakers of change before becoming the agents of change. Despite adverse situations, let's turn our complaints into praise and a positive confession. I will reacquaint myself with the practice of blessing the Lord at all times and letting His praise continually be in my mouth. I will take a sin break and never take a break from praising the Lord despite my circumstances.

Remember that Paul encourages us:

> *"I beseech you therefore, brethren, by the mercies of God, that ye present your bodies a living sacrifice, holy, acceptable unto God, which is your reasonable service. And be not conformed to this world: but be ye transformed by the renewing of your mind, that ye may prove what is that good, and acceptable, and perfect, will of God." (Romans 12:1-2)*

I beseech, beg, encourage, entreat, urge, plead, implore, and appeal to you, brethren, by the mercies of God, that you present your bodies as living sacrifices. This entails making our bodies presents, wrapping them, and placing them out of reach of any and everything.

Transformation to Conformity

On April 16, 2003, just one day before our 20th anniversary, my wife and I purchased our second home in the lovely city of Hercules CA—a brand-new, 5-bedroom, 4-bathroom, 3400-square-foot haven. We had it going on—a TV in every room with DirectTV as our carrier.

One day after work, I went into the family room to watch TV. So, I picked up the remote and turned on the TV, and nothing happened. I tried a few things but still had no luck. I replaced the batteries in the remote, but it still was not working. Then, I went to the downstairs guest room and grabbed the remote that looked exactly like the one in the family room. Back then, the remote only worked with the TV it was programmed for. So, I moved on to the next one. I went to the room where my granddaughter Sa'ryah stays when she comes over. I reasoned that she may have switched them—she is a child, after all. But the TV would not turn on. By the way, please stop trying to conform to someone else's anointing because it looks easy. You will never master it, even if you try to be a copy of someone else. But I digress... Back to the remote.

I had an epiphany: the remote in the family room had been deprogrammed. It had conformed to its generic self, reversed from transformation to conformity. My remote had backslidden. It looked saved but had lost its anointing power to turn on the TV it was meant to operate. I had to get the remote to transform into the TV remote in the family room.

I had to reacquaint this remote to the god of the TV. I hadn't converted a remote in a long time. Could I do it? I had forgotten how to get a remote saved; it had to be born again. I had forgotten how to lead a remote to the Lord; it had been so long since my last conversion. So, I had to pull out the manual to walk me through the transformation process. After I followed the manual's steps, I could convert the remote to its rightful state. The entire house rejoiced over one remote being transformed right before our eyes. It was back in its rightful state to function as it was designed. What is the lesson to be learned from this story? Transformation is not easy, but it is doable and worth every moment!

Metamorphosis

We need to change our behavior toward Christ. Stop saying, "I'm being me."

> *"If any man will come after me, let him deny himself, and take up his cross daily, and follow me." (Luke 9:23)*

True transformation is not a one-day-a-week endeavor; it's a daily commitment to living out our faith in every aspect of our lives. As followers of Christ, we are called to be set apart, a light in the darkness, reflecting His love and grace to the world around us. This means that our pursuit of change must extend beyond Sunday mornings and into every facet of our existence.

We are currently the most infected and the least tested. Therefore, let us take better care of our health. Let's change how we rest, eat, drink, sleep, drive, dress, and communicate. Let's stop being jealous and instead appreciate, celebrate, encourage, promote, and uplift everyone. The late Bishop Otis Lockett said, "What you make happen for others, God will make happen for you!"

The Greek word for transformed is *metamorphoo*. Paul says to be transformed and not conformed. The root word is form—our form, shape, appearance, attitude, and behavior. Some people in church are trying to be like others instead of being like Jesus. We dance the same, sing like each other, preach like each other, and pray like each other.

> **I was born an original and refuse to die a copycat.**

When we dance, let it be because we know it denotes victory. Sing because it tells the devil that no matter what he does, he can't take away our joy. We've been changed! Preach to bring about change! Preach because we're anointed to do it! Pray because it not only keeps us delivered but also keeps us in a state of change! We don't pray enough for God to allow change to occur. We should shout with a triumphant voice because we've been set free.

I admire people and their anointing, but I only want to be like Jesus.

Strategies for Metamorphosis

Transformation is a process that requires intentional effort and practical steps. If you're ready to embark on the journey of change and experience the metamorphosis God has in store for you, consider implementing these strategies:

1. Work on one thing right now.

2. Start now: don't procrastinate.

3. Start small: get a few wins under your belt.

4. Tweak your plan as you go.

5. Have a reason, a why.

6. Write down any obstacles.

7. Know yourself: avoid habits, people, and situations that trigger you.

8. Seek support systems: family, friends, and co-workers.

9. In all your ways, acknowledge God, and He will direct your path (Proverbs 3:6).

10. Stay positive. We can do all things through Christ (Philippians 4:13).

11. Know your player haters and watch for sabotage.

12. Rejoice in the Lord always, and again, I say rejoice (Philippians 4:4).

13. Celebrate little wins with rewards.

14. Get plenty of rest. You need energy to overcome the urges.

15. If you try and fail, regroup and try again.

16. Trust and enjoy the process.

Each day, as you embrace change, trust the process and see it through to the end. The *10 Keys to Maximizing Your Heavenly FICO SCORES Workbook* can guide you. We can all strive to live better and mature into the person God called us to be. Aim to maximize, not just raise, your heavenly FICO SCORES. By refusing to settle for good when better is possible, striving for the best becomes the next step. Let's give our best effort.

Faith is the foundation that moves God and elevates our heavenly FICO SCORES. But it is an ongoing journey, not a one-time event. As we stay focused on God, resist conformity to the world, and embrace the transformative process of change, our faith will grow stronger day by day. We will overcome obstacles, develop new habits, and mature into the fullness of who God created us to be.

It won't always be easy, but as we trust God and enjoy the journey, celebrating victories along the way, we will see our lives and our heavenly standing transformed. Let's set our sights on raising our SCORES and maxing them out for the glory of God and not grow weary in our pursuit of achieving our goal of transformation. As we yield our will and give Him our best through a life of growing, steadfast, unmovable faith and perseverance, He will do exceedingly abundantly above all we could ask or imagine. So, let's embrace the adventure of faith and watch our heavenly FICO SCORES soar to new heights!

It's time to wake up! No more sleeping in bed or wasting days, weeks, months, or years in the same place. We must change and start pursuing the life God has called us to live. We see an example of this when King David writes:

> *"I will bless the LORD at all times: his praise shall continually be in my mouth." (Psalm 34:1)*

This declaration comes from David's escape from Abimelech, the King of the Philistines, as recorded in 1 Samuel 21:10-15. We must choose to speak life, not death, no matter what we face. David understood that praise was a positive confession despite adverse circumstances and recognized the power in our words.

Change is a powerful and necessary part of our journey. It may not always be easy or comfortable, but it is essential for growth and transformation. As we navigate the challenges and opportunities of change, let us keep our eyes fixed on Jesus, the unchanging One who is the same yesterday, today, and forever.

Let's be willing to let go of old mindsets, habits, and behaviors that hold us back and embrace the new things God is doing in our lives. Let us pursue excellence, not for the sake of impressing others but for honoring God and fulfilling His purposes for us.

As we seek first the kingdom of God and His righteousness, we can trust that He will take care of everything else. He will provide for our needs, guide our steps, and empower us to live the abundant life He has in store for us. So, let us approach change with faith, courage, and expectancy. Let us seek God's favor and blessing and believe that our best days are ahead of us and that God is working all things together for our good and His glory.

As we continue this transformation journey, may we experience the joy and freedom that comes from walking in obedience to God and aligning our lives with His perfect will. May we see our heavenly FICO SCORES soar as we trust Him and seek His face above all else.

Remember, you are not alone in this process. God is with you every step of the way, cheering you on and empowering you to become all He has created you to be. Embrace the power of change and watch because He will do exceedingly abundantly above all you could ask or imagine.

CHAPTER 7

Obligation Without Hesitation

"God is not a man, that he should lie; neither the son of man, that he should repent: hath he said, and shall he not do it? or hath he spoken, and shall he not make it good?" (Numbers 23:19)

Whatever God says, He does. He is not like men who make promises they don't intend to keep or change their minds on a whim. When God speaks, His Word is as good as done. As the Psalmist declares, "I will keep my word that I have promised you. I won't break my word; I have spoken" (Psalm 89:34 NIRV). We can trust in the unchanging, unfailing nature of God's promises.

However, we must be discerning to ensure that it is truly God's voice we are hearing, not our desires, the opinions of others, or the deceptive whispers of the enemy. Satan, the master deceiver, is skilled at disguising his lies as truth, making us believe that our thoughts and impulses are from God. We need only look to Eve's experience in the Garden of Eden to see the devastating consequences of listening to the wrong voice. This is why we must cultivate a deep, intimate relationship with Christ, learning to recognize and follow His voice above all others. As Jesus Himself said, "My sheep hear my voice, and I know them, and they follow me" (John 10:27).

The Lord is obligated to keep His Word. He is not like men who give their word but never fulfill it. As I meditated on the word "obligation," the first thing that came to my mind was its similarity to the word "commitment." Obligation and commitment are similar in terms of responsibilities, but they are not identical. Commitment requires dedication, loyalty, wholeheartedness, a pledge of devotion, prioritizing, and sacrificing.

> *"Who keeps an oath even when it hurts, and does not change their mind." (Psalms 15:4 NIV)*

Obligation, on the other hand, is the condition of being morally or legally bound to do something. It is defined as a binding agreement between two or more parties to do or not do something in exchange for something of value. Obligation is similar to being under contract, which is a legally binding agreement between two or more parties. It is best to have all contracts in writing to avoid misunderstandings and to hold all parties accountable.

A Sacred Obligation

In my view, obligation takes commitment to the next level by adding a formal duty or responsibility, often with a contractual agreement. When we make a vow or pledge to the Lord, we are entering into a sacred obligation:

> *"When a man makes a vow to the Lord or takes an oath to obligate himself by a pledge, he must not break his word but must do everything he said." (Numbers 30:2 NIV)*

It is important to understand that when God obligates Himself to keep His Word to us, we, in turn, have a responsibility to uphold our end of the agreement. God's Word will not return void; it will accomplish His purposes and succeed in whatever He sends it to do (Isaiah 55:11). Even if we are faithless, He remains faithful, for He cannot deny Himself (2 Timothy 2:13). Our role is to walk by faith, not by sight (2 Corinthians 5:7), trusting in His promises even when circumstances seem to contradict them.

Unfortunately, many profess faith but resort to walking by sight when challenges arise. We claim to believe God's Word but live as though it doesn't apply to our situation. This is the opposite of what scripture teaches. As Hebrews 10:38 declares, "Now the just shall live by faith: but if any man draw back, my soul shall have no pleasure in him." Those who are righteous in God's sight are obligated not merely to walk by faith occasionally but to live by faith consistently. It is our duty, and if we shrink back from this responsibility, God takes no delight in us.

> *Many profess faith but resort to walking by sight when challenges arise.*

Higher Authorities

The Bible provides clear standards for Christians' civil and social duties, particularly in Romans Chapter 13. Here is my version of this passage.

Let everyone be accountable to the higher authorities, for all authorities come from God. The authorities that be are ordained of God. Whoever is against the authorities is against the decree of God. And those who are against His order shall be held accountable for their actions. For authority is in place for those breaking the rules. Keep doing your part; stay consistent, and you don't have to fear if you do that, which is good. You will have approval. Why? For he is the minister of God to thee for good. But if you work evil, be afraid, for you will not go unpunished. The law was not made for the lawful but for the lawless. So, we need to be accountable not just so we won't be punished but also for conscience's sake. So, for this reason, pay your taxes and debts on time as a representative of God. You need to show an orderly, responsible way of living.

Sadly, many church folks have the worst credit because they don't pay their bills on time, and sometimes their debts end up in collections. As Christians, we are called to respect those deserving of honor, give praise to whom praise is due, and pay what we owe (Romans 13:7). The only debt we should have is the continuing debt to love one another, for love fulfills the requirements of God's law (Romans 13:8). When we love our neighbors as ourselves, we will not commit adultery (if married), fornicate (if single), murder, steal, covet, or bear false witness (Romans 13:9). By walking in love, we satisfy the righteous demands of the law. As we put these principles into practice, our heavenly FICO SCORES will increase exponentially.

If we do what God obligates us to do, He will move on our behalf, and our heavenly FICO SCORES will rise as we commit to fulfilling our obligations. Just as in the natural realm, where paying bills on time and keeping balances low leads to a higher FICO score, so too in the spiritual realm, remaining faithful to our commitments results in increased favor and blessing from God. Let us be diligent in getting out of debt, both naturally and spiritually. Our credit scores are ready and waiting for us to do the right thing so that they can skyrocket. Some individuals attempt to manipulate the system by altering their names and Social Security numbers or by becoming authorized users on someone else's credit to boost their own scores. However, with God, there are no shortcuts. He sees the heart and judges justly.

I remember an old song we used to sing, "I made a vow to the Lord, and I won't take it back. Down on my knees, I made a vow, and I won't take it back. Lord, help me to keep my vow, and I won't take it back."

God is always faithful to His Word and will fulfill His obligations to us if we remain steadfast in our commitment to Him. We cannot ask God for anything if we habitually break our vows. When you make a promise, keep it so you can boldly approach the throne of grace in your time of need (Hebrews 4:16).

Trust and Respect

Keeping our promises, oaths, vows, and obligations is crucial because our word is often all we have. My late pastor, Archie B. Brice, taught me that we need to keep our word to one another because it is the foundation of trust and respect. If you borrow money from someone and promise to pay them back on a specific date, but circumstances prevent you from doing so, you must contact them immediately. Don't avoid them; tell them when you will make good on the debt. They trusted you, and you may need their help again. Your reputation is at stake. We are only as good as our word.

The same principle applies to our relationship with God. If we try to avoid our obligations to Him, He is not bound to fulfill His promises to us because we have broken faith. God will never break His Word and He expects us to keep ours. Jesus said:

> "Ye have not chosen me, but I have chosen you, and ordained you, that ye should go and bring forth fruit, and that your fruit should remain: that whatsoever ye shall ask of the Father in my name, he may give it to you. These things I command you, that ye love one another." (John 15:16-17)

Our lives are full of obligations that require us to be at certain places at specific times, prepared to fulfill our duties. Colored People Time (CP Time) "ain't gone cut it"—and I've found that other races use CP time to describe their own race (lol). The point is that tardiness and lack of preparation communicate a lack of respect for others and for the commitments we have made. Showing up on time and ready to engage is a basic form of loving our neighbors.

Being prepared is critical to meeting our obligations with excellence. This means planning ahead, making sure we have everything we need, and leaving early enough to arrive on time. My mother used to say, "Early to bed, early to rise, keeps a person healthy and wise." She would wake us up with a cheerful, "Rise! Shine! Give God the glory, glory," reminding us to thank Him for a new day and to get moving since we had places to be. The early bird gets the worm, as the saying goes. When we prepare in advance, we can respond calmly and effectively to the inevitable surprises life throws our way rather than panicking and reacting.

The Chaos of Poor Planning

Preparation applies to all areas of life—school, work, church, travel, special events, and even mundane tasks like paying bills. By mapping out our days and weeks ahead of time, we insulate ourselves from the chaos of poor planning. We're also better equipped to handle the unexpected, like emergency phone calls from family or friends in need. Having some savings set aside gives us the flexibility to be generous when others need our help without putting our obligations at risk.

When we fail to plan and arrive late or unprepared, we send the message that we're not truly committed, that we're just showing up to avoid penalties or embarrassment. The things that matter most to us should be our top priorities, not our last-minute leftovers.

Many people treat their spiritual lives this way, relegating practices like prayer, Bible study, worship, giving, and self-care to the lowest priority until a crisis hits. Suddenly, when the doctor gives a bad report or finances crumble, they're in church every time the doors are open, begging for prayer. Sadly, their loved ones also suffer, bearing the burden of their unpreparedness. It's much better to make our spiritual and relational health a top priority now, building a solid foundation for the storms of life.

It's time to stop living from one miracle to the next, one government bailout to another, leaving the most important things to chance while we pursue comfort and pleasure. What if, instead, we gave our highest energy and attention to developing our character, our faith, and our God-given purpose, trusting Him to provide for our needs as we put first things first? This is the essence of Matthew 6:33, "But seek ye first the kingdom of God, and his righteousness, and all these things shall be added unto you."

When we make our relationship with God our primary focus and organize our lives around His priorities, Scripture promises that everything else will fall into place. This doesn't mean a trouble-free life, but it means we can face challenges from a place of peace, knowing our foundation is sure. We learn to be proactive rather than reactive, taking responsibility for our spiritual, physical, financial, and relational health. Instead of waiting for others to bail us out, we "work out [our] own salvation with fear and trembling" (Philippians 2:12), doing what we can and trusting God to do what only He can do.

This is the heart of obligation: taking ownership of what God has entrusted to us and stewarding it well. It's not about earning salvation or twisting God's arm to get what we want. It's about living in grateful response to His grace, knowing that He rewards those who diligently seek Him (Hebrews 11:6). It's about the joy of partnering with Him in His purposes, experiencing the abundant life Jesus came to give us (John 10:10).

As we lean into our obligation to God and pursue His kingdom first, we open the door for supernatural transformation in every area of our lives. We develop holy habits that position us for success, like diligence in prayer and studying God's Word, wise financial management, and healthy self-care. We learn to speak faith-filled words that call into existence the promises of God, not the problems of our past or present (Romans 4:17). As we abide in Christ and allow His Word to abide in us, we can ask what we desire and see it come to pass (John 15:7), not because we're perfect but because we're plugged into the Source of all power and provision.

Heavenly Security

In the Gospel of St. Luke 16:1-13, Jesus shared a parable about a rich man and his steward, who was accused of mismanaging the estate. The rich man gave the steward a chance to explain before firing him. Knowing his dismissal was imminent, the steward devised a plan to secure his future by reducing the debts of those who owed the estate, hoping they would help him after he was fired.

The rich man commended the steward, not for his dishonesty, but for his shrewdness. Jesus used this story to teach that the people of the world are often wiser in dealing with their own kind than the children of light. He encouraged his disciples to be generous with their material possessions so that they would be welcomed into eternal dwellings.

Jesus emphasizes that those who are faithful with little will also be faithful with much, and those who are dishonest with little will be dishonest with much. He teaches that if we are not trustworthy with worldly wealth, we cannot be trusted with true riches. This aligns with Jesus' teaching in Matthew 6:19-21, 33, where He advises laying up treasures in Heaven rather than on Earth and seeking God's kingdom first.

This parable teaches the importance of being shrewd and strategic in our dealings, but always with integrity and faithfulness. It reminds us to be generous and to prioritize our spiritual obligations over material ones, ensuring that our actions in this life align with the values of the kingdom of God. The principle is that faithfulness in small things, particularly in the stewardship of earthly resources, demonstrates our readiness to be entrusted with true spiritual riches.

Jesus concludes:

> *"No servant can serve two masters: for either he will hate the one, and love the other; or else he will hold to the one, and despise the other. Ye cannot serve God and mammon." (Luke 16:13)*

In other words, our ultimate allegiance must be to God alone. Money is a tool to be used for His purposes, not a competing master to be served. Where our treasure is, there will our hearts be also (Luke 12:34).

> *"Lay not up for yourselves treasures upon earth, where moth and rust doth corrupt, and where thieves break through and steal: But lay up for yourselves treasures in heaven, where neither moth nor rust doth corrupt, and where thieves do not break through nor steal: For where your treasure is, there will your heart be also." (Matthew 6:19-21, 33)*

Here, Jesus reminds us that our ultimate treasure and security are found not in earthly possessions but in our relationship with God and the eternal rewards that come from putting His kingdom first. When we focus on accumulating wealth and material things, we open ourselves up to the constant threat of loss, whether through natural decay, theft, or the simple fact that we can't take it with us when we die. But when we invest our time, energy, and resources into God's purposes, we store up treasures in Heaven that can never be stolen or destroyed.

This doesn't mean we shouldn't plan for the future or be wise stewards of the resources God has given us. What it does mean is that our primary focus and affection should be on things above, not on things below. It means trusting God to provide for our needs as we put His righteousness and His will above our desires and agendas. It means holding loosely to the things of this world, always ready to use them for His glory rather than our gratification.

> **Our ultimate allegiance must be to God alone.**

When we seek God's kingdom first, we align our priorities with His and experience the freedom that comes from knowing our lives are hidden with Christ in God (Colossians 3:3). We no longer have to strive for significance or security through worldly measures of success because our identity and inheritance are secure in Him. We can afford to be generous, knowing that God owns it all and promises to supply all our needs according to His riches in glory (Philippians 4:19).

Paradigm Shift

This shift in perspective transforms the way we view our obligations and responsibilities. Instead of seeing them as burdens or obstacles to our fulfillment, we see them as opportunities to demonstrate our love for God and others, to grow in faith and faithfulness, and to participate in God's redemptive work in the world. We find joy in the journey, knowing that every act of obedience and sacrifice is an investment in eternity, a chance to experience more of God's life and love flowing through us.

As we commit to putting God first in every area of life, including our finances, time, and relationships, He promises to provide everything we need to fulfill our purpose and enjoy abundant life. This doesn't mean a trouble-free existence, but we can face every challenge confidently, knowing our heavenly Father is faithful and His grace is sufficient.

The key is learning to live as sons and daughters, not orphans. Orphans have to fend for themselves, hoard resources, and strive for security apart from God. Sons and daughters know they are loved, provided for, and called to a purpose greater than themselves. They can afford to be generous, trusting the Father to replenish their supply as they pour out to others. They don't have to fear lack or failure because their identity and inheritance are secure in Christ.

This is the abundant life Jesus invites us into—a life of faith, freedom, and fruitfulness, where every obligation becomes an opportunity to experience and express the love of God. As we embrace our high calling as stewards of His grace, we will see our heavenly FICO SCORES soar, not because we're striving to earn His favor but because we're learning to *live from* His favor, walking in obedience and letting His life flow through us to a world in need.

So, let us not shrink back from the holy obligations God has entrusted to us, but let us press in with faith and faithfulness, knowing that He who began a good work in us will be faithful to complete it (Philippians 1:6). Let us give ourselves fully to the work of the Lord, knowing that our labor is not in vain (1 Corinthians 15:58). And let us fix our eyes on Jesus, the author and finisher of our faith, who for the joy set before Him endured the cross, despising its shame, and is now seated at the right hand of the throne of God (Hebrews 12:2).

As we follow in His footsteps, we will find that every sacrifice is worth it; every act of obedience is an invitation to experience more of His life and love. We will discover that the abundant life is not a destination but a daily journey of faith and faithfulness, one step at a time. And we will see our heavenly FICO SCORES rise, not as an end in themselves but as a byproduct of a life well-lived, a life hidden with Christ in God (Colossians 3:3).

May we be found faithful, not just in the big moments but in the small, unseen choices that make up a life of devotion. May we be quick to obey, slow to make excuses, and eager to embrace the adventures God has in store for us. May we experience the joy of knowing that, no matter what challenges come our way, we are never alone and never without hope, for we serve a God who is faithful to all His promises and able to do exceedingly abundantly above all we could ask or imagine (Ephesians 3:20).

This is the life of obligation without hesitation—a life of faith, obedience, and expectancy, rooted in the faithfulness of God and the finished work of Christ. Let us embrace it with all our hearts, knowing that every act of obedience is an investment in eternity, and every sacrifice is a seed that will yield a harvest of righteousness and peace. And let us encourage one another daily to stay the course, fight the good fight, and finish the race until we hear those precious words from our Savior's lips, "Well done, good and faithful servant. Enter into the joy of your Lord" (Matthew 25:23).

CHAPTER 8

Righteousness Is a Choice

Righteousness, or right standing with God, is often viewed as an unattainable standard or a status reserved for the spiritual elite. However, the truth is that righteousness is a choice available to every believer through faith in Jesus Christ. This chapter will explore the concept of righteousness and how it impacts our heavenly FICO SCORES. We'll examine the difference between self-righteousness and the righteousness that comes from God, the role of grace in our pursuit of righteousness, and the importance of making daily choices that align with God's will. As we choose to walk in righteousness, we'll experience a more profound sense of peace, purpose, and intimacy with God.

> *"And be found in him, not having mine own righteousness, which is of the law, but that which is through the faith of Christ, the righteousness which is of God by faith."*
>
> *(Philippians 3:9 DRF)*

Righteousness is to have integrity both morally and spiritually—a virtuous characteristic that not many hold. It is an honest lifestyle complete with ethical soundness, even when no one is watching. Righteousness is to be righteous, just, upright, and correct. It is a lifestyle anyone can choose, but sadly, many will not push themselves to live at this level. As

Paul said in Philippians 3:14, "I press toward the mark for the prize of the high calling of God in Christ Jesus." Everything unrighteous is sin to God.

It is easy to cut corners and just get by; we have all done it at some point. However, there comes a time when we must all say to ourselves, "Enough is enough." Cutting corners does not get us ahead. In fact, it sets us back and ensures that we are never truly prepared, always looking for the next shortcut. We should stay mentally and spiritually focused, moving forward as if all of Heaven were watching. And believe me, all of Heaven is watching. Proverbs 15:3 says, "The eyes of the LORD are in every place, beholding the evil and the good."

It's a Choice

So, should we walk in righteousness or not? This is a question that only we can answer individually. No one can or will force us to live right or wrong—not other people, not the devil, not even God Himself. We alone determine our fate through the choices we make. It's that simple— to walk in righteousness or not is entirely up to us.

Everyone will face challenging circumstances in life when we least expect it. There's no way around it. However, regardless of the situation, we have the final say in how we respond—either negatively or positively—by choosing to walk uprightly.

> *"But seek ye first the kingdom of God, and his righteousness; and all these things shall be added unto you." (Matthew 6:33)*

Let's break this verse down. Seek first the kingdom of God means prioritizing God's righteousness and His way of doing things above all else. Romans 14:17 tells us, "For the kingdom of God is not meat and drink; but righteousness, and peace, and joy in the Holy Ghost." The kingdom of God is not about external things or worldly pursuits but about living in right standing with God and experiencing the peace and joy that comes from His presence in our lives. The kingdom of God must take precedence over everything in our lives through prayer, repentance, worship, praise, adoration, thanksgiving, and studying the Word of God.

> **This is not our own righteousness but HIS righteousness.**

It's about not veering off the path but staying in right alignment with His Word.

"For therein is the righteousness of God revealed from faith to faith: as it is written, the just shall live by faith." (Romans 1:17)

Back to Matthew 6:33 (NIV) "And all these things shall be added unto you" refers to everything that people obsess over—food, drink, clothes, and the constant pursuit of more and more material things that moth, rust, and thieves can ruin or steal. Matthew 6:34 goes on to say, "Therefore do not worry about tomorrow, for tomorrow will worry about itself. Each day has enough trouble of its own."

We choose to live in such a way that God can use us anywhere and anytime, regardless of the difficulties and setbacks we face that make us want to throw in the towel or take shortcuts. It's often when we go through trials—when we are at our weakest and ready to quit—that His strength is perfected in us and put on display for all the world to see. In those moments, we overcome not by our own power or might but by the Spirit of God.

Romans 8:31 asks, "If God be for us, who can be against us?" Take the first letter off "AGAINST," the "A," and the last two letters, "ST," and you have a word in the middle: "GAIN." Who doesn't want you to gain? The devil. He can and does present situations, but he does not determine the outcome. You facilitate the outcome by what you choose to do, whether right or wrong. Even doing nothing is a choice that determines the outcome, like taking your hands off the steering wheel and closing your eyes to the situation.

God's Servant Job

Let's take a look at the story of Job, a righteous man who experienced more losses in a single day than most people face in a lifetime. God allowed Satan to strip Job of all his worldly possessions *and* his children, saying, in essence, "Go ahead, Satan, and watch as I get the glory out of Job's story." God knew that Job would not let Him down. With practice and prayer, you and I can be the same. Job had the highest heavenly FICO SCORES I've ever seen.

> *"There was a man named Job, living in the land of Uz, who worshiped God and was faithful to him. He was a good man, careful not to do anything evil. He had seven sons and three daughters, and owned seven thousand sheep, three thousand camels, one thousand head of cattle, and five hundred donkeys. He also had a large number of servants and was the richest man in the East. Job's sons used to take turns giving a feast, to which all the others would come, and they always invited their three sisters to join them. The morning after each feast, Job would get up early and offer sacrifices for each of his children in order to purify them. He always did this because he thought that one of them might have sinned by insulting God unintentionally."*
>
> *(Job 1:1-5 GNT)*

The Bible tells us that one day, the sons of God came to present themselves before the Lord and Satan also came among them. Up to that point, Satan had been having great success, turning the hearts of the people away from God.

In my mind, I picture Satan walking in with the rest of the sons of God. The Lord asked him, "Where have you been? What have you been doing with yourself?" Now, all the attention was on Satan. He answered boastfully, "I've been walking back and forth, roaming the earth, seeking whom I may overwhelm and devour." I can imagine him laughing as he recounted how he had made one person give up because of misfortune, another throw in the towel because of job loss, another quit because of divorce, and others living in depression due to heartbreak or the loss of loved ones. I picture him talking about how gullible people are and how easy it is to get them to sell their souls for the love of money.

He can't stop laughing at mankind's predicament, mocking the weak, unmotivated, undisciplined, and nonchalant attitude of God's people in the face of challenges and the threat of losing their possessions. He states, "I've led billions astray without resistance. They willingly give in to the allure of wealth, fame, power, recognition, respect, beauty, and glamour. There isn't a single person you created that I can't break and make curse you!"

Then God speaks up, saying, "Yeah, I know you've deceived many— those who cut corners, don't fast and pray, study their Bibles, or gather together with other believers. But don't get it twisted. You deceived the hearers, not the doers. The ones who talk about faith but walk by sight, the ones suffering from an identity crisis, the uncommitted ones, the ones who disobey My Word, the ones uninterested in sanctification, the ones too impatient to wait for their change, the ones not pursuing excellence, stewardship, breakthrough, and deliverance. Those who quit in the night, weeping, unable to understand how joy comes in the morning.

Weeping and complaining represent the night; joy and praise represent the morning. Praise is a positive confession in spite of negative situations." (Let me stop preaching and get back to the story!)

Then God name-drops: "Have you considered my servant Job? There is no one on earth more perfect and upright, faithful and just. He worships Me, has integrity, and stays true to his calling. He doesn't cut corners when it comes to praising and worshiping Me, and he is careful not to do anything evil."

Satan replied, "Yeah, I saw him, and I saw how much You have blessed him. He's blessed in the city, blessed in the fields, blessed everywhere he goes. Do You really believe he'd worship You if he didn't have all the things You've given him? You've covered and smothered him with Your lovingkindness, goodness, and mercy. He's got Your protection and direction over his family and everything he owns. Come on, Lord, You've given him everything and even enlarged his territory. He prays, and You keep increasing him. But just suppose You took away everything he has. He would curse You to Your face!"

In my mind, I can see the Lord saying, "WHAT! You've lost your mind, Satan. It's not about the stuff; it's about who he is." I envision Satan replying, "Yeah, right. Okay, that's Your claim, but I've been breaking down your people with no resistance." It's right here in my imagination where I see God saying, "Enough of this banter." If He were a betting man, He might say, "All right, I'll take you up on that challenge. Everything he has is in your power, but you better not harm him." So, with God's permission, Satan leaves to do his work, knowing he can't act against anyone without God's approval.

On a day when Job's children were having a feast at the eldest brother's home, a series of messengers came running to Job, each bearing devastating news. The first reported that the Sabeans had attacked and stolen all the oxen and donkeys, killing all the servants except him. Before he had finished speaking, another servant came and said that lightning had struck the sheep and shepherds, killing them all, with only him escaping. Then another servant arrived, saying that three bands of Chaldean raiders had taken the camels and killed all the servants, with only him surviving. Finally, a fourth messenger came and reported that a tornado had swept in from the desert, collapsing the house where Job's children were feasting, killing them all, with only him escaping to deliver the news. Bad news travels fast.

Job did not sin by blaming God.

Upon hearing this, Job got up, tore his clothes in grief, shaved his head, and threw himself face down on the ground, worshiping the Lord. He said, "I was born with nothing, and I will die with nothing. The Lord gave, and now He has taken away. Blessed be the name of the Lord." Despite all the terrible things that happened to him in rapid succession, Job did not sin by blaming God. He was deeply hurt, grieved, and possibly angry, but he never sinned or blamed God.

In the second chapter, the sons of God and Satan present themselves before the Lord again. God and Satan basically repeat the same dialogue, with God trying to get Satan to admit that he did not succeed in getting Job to curse Him. God asks Satan, "Where have you been? What have you been up to?" Satan responds, "Walking up and down in the earth, having my way with Your people, as I always do." The Lord then said to Satan, "What happened with My servant Job? I told you he had 850 FICO SCORES with Me, and there is none like him on Earth—a perfect and upright man, one who reverences Me and stays clear of you and your shenanigans. Even after I allowed you to take everything from him without cause, he still holds fast to his integrity." Satan replied, "Yes, but if you took his health—skin for skin, bones and flesh—he will curse You to Your face."

I know God doesn't bet, but if He did, I can imagine Him saying, "Double or nothing, Satan. He is in your hands, but do not kill him." So, Satan left and struck Job with agonizing, painful sores and boils from head to toe. Job took a piece of broken pottery and scraped his skin to relieve the pain and remove the boils.

Job was in such a terrible state that even his wife asked him, "What's wrong with you? Why are you still holding on to your integrity? Curse God and die!" But he responded, telling her that she was speaking foolishly. "Should I only walk in righteousness when things are going well?" Job did not sin with his lips but maintained his integrity.

Even when his three friends came to visit, they did not recognize Job and sat with him for seven days before anyone spoke. When they finally did speak, they all accused Job of sinning, suggesting that this was his payback and that perhaps even his children had sinned. But just because someone is going through hardship doesn't mean it's because they have been unrighteous. Everything in life is a test to see how we will respond, which is why we must not cut corners in our pursuit of a righteous life.

Double for His Trouble

The Book of Job is a fascinating story of how we should learn to persevere and never give up. As Job declared, "Though He slay me, yet will I trust Him" (Job 13:15). Even in our grief, we must remember that weeping may endure for a night, but joy comes in the morning. Job knew that his Redeemer lived and would ultimately vindicate him. God got the glory from Job's story and gave him double for his trouble. Even though God had to correct him, He still blessed him.

At the end of the Book of Job, in chapter 42, we see that Job prayed for his three friends, and the Lord restored his fortunes, giving him twice as much as he had before. Job's brothers, sisters, and former friends came to visit him, feasting with him in his house. They expressed their sympathy and comforted him for all his troubles, each giving him money and a gold ring.

The Lord blessed the latter part of Job's life even more than the first. Job ended up with fourteen thousand sheep, six thousand camels, two thousand oxen, and one thousand donkeys. He also had seven more sons and three more daughters. We need to pass our tests and go through our trials and tribulations so we can receive our blessings. If we never mature and weather the storms of life, we are doomed to repeat these tests over and over until we mature and go through. Going through means just that—going through so you can come out better, not bitter; stronger, not weaker; and wiser, not foolish.

From Job's story, we learn that righteous living is the only way to live. Proverbs 14:34 says, "Righteousness exalts a nation, but sin is a reproach to any people." Living righteously elevates anyone's heavenly FICO SCORES. God shows no partiality. Sin will drag you down, lower your SCORES, degrade you, diminish you, humble you, and embarrass you if you try to cut corners. When pressure comes, it will expose you if you've been living a lie. But if we live in righteousness, when pressure comes, we will be prepared and ready for the moment, and we will be exalted, not demoted. You can do it. Your success in God depends on it!

> "If any man be in Christ, he is a new creature: unrighteous living is no longer a part of him; behold, he has become new in righteousness." (2 Corinthians 5:17 DRF)

The Grace to Live Right
As we navigate the challenges of life, it's essential to remember that our righteousness is not based on our own merits but on the finished work

of Christ. When we place our faith in Him, we are clothed in His righteousness, which far surpasses anything we could achieve through our own efforts (Philippians 3:9). This doesn't mean we have a license to sin; rather, it means we have the power to live uprightly because of the grace He has given us.

In fact, as we abide in Christ and allow His Word to abide in us, we will naturally bear the fruit of righteousness (John 15:4-5). This fruit is not something we can manufacture through sheer willpower but is the result of the Holy Spirit's work in our lives as we surrender to His leading. As we walk in the Spirit, we will not gratify the desires of the flesh but will instead exhibit love, joy, peace, patience, kindness, goodness, faithfulness, gentleness, and self-control (Galatians 5:16, 22-23).

Of course, this doesn't mean we will never stumble or make mistakes. We are still human, and we will face temptations and trials. However, when we do sin, we have an advocate with the Father—Jesus Christ, the righteous One (1 John 2:1). When we confess our sins, He is faithful and just to forgive us and cleanse us from all unrighteousness (1 John 1:9). This is not an excuse to take sin lightly but a reminder of the incredible grace and mercy available to us when we humbly acknowledge our need for Him.

As we grow in righteousness, we will find that our priorities begin to shift. Instead of chasing after temporal pleasures and worldly accolades, we will seek first the kingdom of God and His righteousness (Matthew 6:33). We will begin to view our time, talents, and resources as gifts from God to be used for His glory and the good of others. We will be more concerned with storing up treasures in Heaven than accumulating wealth on earth (Matthew 6:19-20).

This doesn't mean we have to take a vow of poverty or neglect our earthly responsibilities. In fact, God often blesses us materially so that we can be a blessing to others (Genesis 12:2). However, it does mean holding everything we have with an open hand, recognizing that it all belongs to Him and is to be used according to His purposes. It means being faithful stewards of what He has entrusted to us, whether much or little (Luke 16:10-11).

Ultimately, living a life of righteousness is about aligning our will with God's and allowing Him to conform us to the image of His Son (Romans 8:29). It's about dying to self and living for Christ, knowing that in losing our life for His sake, we actually find it (Matthew 16:25). It's about persevering through trials and tribulations, knowing that the testing of our faith produces endurance and character (James 1:2-4).

As we walk in righteousness, we can have confidence that our heavenly FICO SCORES are soaring, not because of our own goodness but because of the goodness of the One who gave His life for us. We can rest assured that He who began a good work in us will carry it on to completion until the day of Christ Jesus (Philippians 1:6).

So, let us press on toward the goal to win the prize for which God has called us heavenward in Christ Jesus (Philippians 3:14). Let us lay aside every weight and the sin that so easily entangles us. Let us run with endurance the race set before us, fixing our eyes on Jesus, the author and perfecter of our faith (Hebrews 12:1-2). And let us encourage one another daily, as long as it is called "today," so that none of us may be hardened by sin's deceitfulness (Hebrews 3:13).

As we do this, we will experience the abundant life that Jesus promised—not a life free from trouble but a life filled with His peace, joy, and purpose (John 10:10). We will be able to say with Paul, "I have fought the good fight. I have finished the race. I have kept the faith. Now there is in store for me the crown of righteousness, which the Lord, the Righteous Judge, will award to me on that day—and not only to me but also to all who have longed for His appearing" (2 Timothy 4:7-8).

May we all be found faithful, walking in the righteousness that comes through faith in Christ, and may our heavenly FICO SCORES continue to rise as we trust in Him and follow His leading. For in Him, we have everything we need for life and godliness (2 Peter 1:3). In Him, we are more than conquerors (Romans 8:37). And in Him, we have the hope of eternal life—a hope that does not disappoint, because God's love has been poured out into our hearts through the Holy Spirit, who has been given to us (Romans 5:5).

CHAPTER 9

You Can Excel

Excellence is a term often associated with perfection, but the reality is that excellence is a journey, not a destination. It's not about being flawless or achieving a specific status; instead, it's about consistently striving to be better and making the most of the talents and opportunities God has given us.

In this chapter, we will explore the concept of excellence through the lens of spiritual growth and discover how anyone can excel in their walk with God, ultimately leading to an increase in their heavenly FICO SCORES. We'll look at examples from scripture and everyday life to illustrate that excellence is not about perfection but about progress, persistence, and faithfulness in our pursuit of God's will for our lives.

I chose the word "excel" over "excellent." To be excellent is subjective and can vary from person to person and system to system; it has too many variables. Baseball Hall of Fame player Ty Cobb's career batting average was .366; Ted Williams' was .344; Babe Ruth's was .342; and Hank Aaron's was .305. All of them were inducted into the Hall of Fame, and none had a batting average over .400. Out of 10 times at bat, not one could average 4 hits. But they all excelled.

"And be not conformed to this world: but be ye transformed by the renewing of your mind, that ye may prove what is that good, and acceptable, and perfect, will of God." (Romans 12:2)

My favorite boxer growing up was Muhammad Ali. He talked a lot of smack and backed it up most of the time. He did not win every fight, but he did excel by winning most of the fights and the hearts of the people. He was considered the greatest heavyweight fighter of all time. This, of course, is subjective. But in my humble opinion, he was. He never conformed but transformed and transcended 20th-century culture.

He won the heavyweight gold medal at the 1960 Olympic Games in Rome. In 1964, he transformed his slave name, Cassius Clay, Jr., into Muhammad Ali. He refused to conform and fight in the Vietnam War. He was stripped of his heavyweight belt but was able to regain the title two more times during his career. When I got to high school during the 1975/1976 season, a young Sugar Ray Leonard won the gold medal in the 1976 Olympics in Montreal, Canada. He had a similar style to Muhammad Ali while fighting as a welterweight, 147 pounds—quick hands and feet.

Growing up in Richmond, CA, I used that same style whenever I got into fights. I'd jab and use a flurry of quick punches. I never took myself as bad or brave enough to try boxing at a gym, and we didn't have the money anyway. But whenever I got into a fight, which I never started when someone hit me first, it was on. Let's go! I got very good at using Ali and Leonard's fighting styles, but I never excelled or perfected my craft. You may say I was, at best, a question mark, a what if, a could've-should've-would've. I conformed to my environment instead of transforming. Scripture tells us not to conform to the norms of the times but to transform by renewing our minds. In my neighborhood, everyone conformed. Significantly, few ever transformed.

Jack of All Trades

Growing up, I would hear the saying, "Jack of all trades but master of none." The correct phrase is, "A jack of all trades is a master of none, but oftentimes better than a master of one." It can be applied to males or females; while someone may not be an expert in a single field, having a wide range of skills and knowledge can be even more valuable. Their skills and abilities to adapt to different situations emphasize the benefits of being well-rounded and adaptable.

However, where I grew up, the phrase was used to describe someone negatively. The jack could sort of fix or do anything but never excelled in anything they claimed to be able to do. From fixing your car engine, carburetor, brakes, water pump, and even bodywork to pulling out dents, painting the car, and doing it all. If you have a house in need of electrical, plumbing, roofing, carpentry, or painting—it doesn't matter. The jack claimed to be able to do it all and was great at selling you on that fact. I have to hand it to them; they were great starters, taking things apart but not putting them back together the way they came apart. You'd find screws, parts lying around as if they were not needed to finish the job. Often, before the job was complete, the jack would take off with your money and start another job somewhere else, never completing your job. Or if the job were completed a few days or weeks later, you'd have to call someone else to correct the work. These jacks could sort of do many things, but none were done excellently. They cut corners and didn't have the skills to excel in the task.

"A jack of all trades" was initially used to describe William Shakespeare, a playwright who always hung around theaters. It was said he helped with the stage, the wardrobe, and the set. He remembered lines and even tried to direct. And he was good at everything he did. The term "a jack of all trades" was, in fact, a compliment—but just not in my neighborhood.

We break the cycle by mastering the fundamentals of the one thing we are passionate about before moving on to the next. Most people get distracted by attempting to excel at multiple things at once. Then what happens? We end up excelling at nothing and becoming mediocre at best in everything.

To excel in any arena requires focus, attention to detail, persistence, and determination. Running into speed bumps is inevitable, so slow down and focus! Roadblocks come to block us, so pay attention!

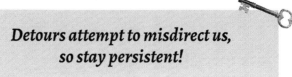

Detours attempt to misdirect us, so stay persistent!

Pitfalls are all around trying to stop us, but we must keep our determination!

Isaiah reminds us:

> *"No weapon that is formed against thee shall prosper; and every tongue that shall rise against thee in judgment thou shalt condemn." (Isaiah 54:17)*

Embrace the Journey

We must remain focused to achieve our desired results. Even when setbacks hit and we stumble and fall, we must get back up again and again and continue our journey to achieve. The acronym for JOURNEY is Just Open Up, Right's Never Easy, Yield! Everyone is not trying to excel on their journey! The average person is mediocre, frustrated, upset, has no clue, is not paying attention, and seeks to be entertained while playing the victim card to escape the reality of life. We don't pray as God requires.

We stop fasting for deliverance. We don't study the Word of God to know who and why we are.

No more. Let's stop excelling in social media and start excelling in the things of God. We start by seeking the kingdom of God and His righteousness so all the things we see others with on social media and all around us can be added unto us. We've got it twisted. We need to start majoring and excelling in the things of God so the minor things of life can be added unto us. God is not looking for excellence. He's looking for obedience. Millions are average, but we don't have to be. We can excel and become more than conquerors because if God is for us, who can be against us? Who is against our gaining? Who or whatever we allow to distract us.

Begin to excel and achieve the things of God. We'll catch His attention, and He will take care of our needs. As a result, our heavenly FICO SCORES will rise. The average person is more interested in being entertained than finding their purpose, challenging themselves to increase in wisdom, knowledge, and grace. They can only find happiness by watching everyone else excel and win in life, watching others live the life they can only dream about, getting out of debt, owning new cars, and living in nice houses. At the same time, they remain stuck in a rut with no plan, no get-up-and-go, no motivation, no dreams, and no vision. It's time to wake up. No more sleeping in bed. No more wasting days, weeks, months, or years in the same place. Most people will never excel and raise their heavenly FICO SCORES. You and I must not be among the millions who will never transform.

How Jabez Excelled

Let's review the story of Jabez and how he believed his destiny was greater than his current circumstances. Watch how Jabez's prayer and life choices demonstrate that anyone can excel and achieve great things when they seek God and His righteousness. Jabez comes from a lineage of praise. His story is a perfect case study of someone who could have given up and conformed to his environment. But Jabez knew there was more to his life, and he understood that his destiny was greater than his current condition. So, he went to God and sought Him regarding his position in life:

> *"And Jabez was more honorable than his brethren: and his mother called his name Jabez, saying, Because I bare him with sorrow. And Jabez called on the God of Israel, saying, Oh that thou wouldest bless me indeed, and enlarge my coast, and that thine hand might be with me, and that thou wouldest keep me from evil, that it may not grieve me! And God granted him that which he requested." (1 Chronicles 4:9-10)*

Jabez's story teaches us several valuable lessons about excelling in life:

1. We must walk with honor and respect, not allowing the labels placed on us by others to define us. Even if these labels are given to us at birth by our parents or any other person, we must not let negative labels or the way they make us feel cause us to conform. We must break away from the norm and let nothing stop us from walking in integrity and honor. Consider this: Jabez was more honorable than his brothers, but what labels did their mother give them that caused them to conform to those labels? Perhaps she labeled them as disappointments, pathetic, useless, no good, just like their father—a nobody. Remember, you can surpass people's labels. It doesn't matter what others say about you; rise above your situation and mistakes. As long as you have breath, you can excel in God. Wear the label of Philippians 4:13, which says, "I can do all things through Christ which strengtheneth me" and Romans 8:37, "Nay, in all these things we are more than conquerors through him that loved us."

2. Jabez was wise enough to understand that his predicament required more than just honor. He understood the principle in Matthew 6:33, which tells us, "But seek ye first the kingdom of God, and His righteousness; and all these things shall be added unto you." Seeking God's righteousness first opens the door for us to ask God for what we truly need and want.

3. Jabez called upon the name of the Lord. No matter what we face, we must know where our help comes from. We have to become sick and tired of being sick and tired. We must stop reacting to trouble and sorrow and start responding to God's call for our lives. You may have difficult relationships with people who don't understand and talk about you but learn how to develop a great relationship with God by seeking Him first. You can't force people to love you—money can't buy love, and dinner and flowers won't fix love. You can't make people respect you; you must give respect to receive respect. So, first and foremost, learn to respect yourself.

4. Just as Jabez was specific with his petition to God, we must also be specific when approaching the throne of grace. He asked for blessings, increase, expansion, favor, protection, and peace. And guess what? God granted him everything he requested.

Romans 2:11 says, "For there is no respect of persons with God." God loves you just as much as He loved Jabez and wants to give you the desires of your heart. As you move forward, excel in seeking God first to maximize your heavenly FICO SCORES. Remember, God desires to give you the desires of your heart.

Excellence is not about perfection but consistently pursuing growth and improvement. It's about using the gifts and opportunities God has given us to impact the world and bring glory to His name.

To excel in our walk with God, we must prioritize our relationship with Him above all else. This means investing time in prayer, studying His Word, and seeking His will for our lives. As we do this, we will find that God begins to transform us from the inside out, molding us into the image of Christ and empowering us to live a life of excellence.

> **We must prioritize our relationship with Him above all else.**

Keep Pressing Forward

The apostle Paul understood this principle well:

> *"Brethren, I count not myself to have apprehended: but this one thing I do, forgetting those things which are behind, and reaching forth unto those things which are before, I press toward the mark for the prize of the high calling of God in Christ Jesus."*
> *(Philippians 3:13-14)*

Paul recognized that the key to excelling in his walk with God was to keep pressing forward, forgetting past mistakes, and focusing on the goal. He didn't allow his past to define him but instead chose to pursue the high calling of God in Christ Jesus.

Like Paul, we can excel in our spiritual lives by keeping our eyes fixed on Jesus and pressing forward in faith. We can let go of past failures and mistakes and embrace the new life and opportunities God has for us.

As we pursue excellence in our walk with God, our heavenly FICO SCORES will begin to soar. We will experience a deeper intimacy with

God, a greater sense of purpose and fulfillment, and an increased capacity to make a difference in our world.

So, let us approach excellence not as a destination but as a lifelong journey of growth and transformation. Let us seek God's blessing and favor, walk in honor and integrity, and believe in His love and desire to bless us. And let us keep pressing forward, knowing that as we do, we will experience the abundant life God has in store for us.

Remember, anyone can excel in their walk with God. It doesn't matter where you've been or what you've done; what matters is where you're going and what you're doing now. Embrace the lessons from Jabez's life, apply them to your own, and watch as God begins to do exceedingly, abundantly, above all you could ask or think (Ephesians 3:20).

May your pursuit of excellence bring glory to God and lead you to a life of purpose, fulfillment, and intimate relationship with Him. And may your heavenly FICO SCORES soar as you seek His kingdom and righteousness first, trusting that all these things will be added unto you (Matthew 6:33).

CHAPTER 10

The Responsibility of Stewardship

"Let a man so account of us, as of the ministers of Christ, and stewards of the mysteries of God. Moreover it is required in stewards, that a man be found faithful." (1 Corinthians 4:1-2)

In its simplest form, stewardship is managing, supervising, or serving. It is important to note that stewardship does not imply ownership. A steward carefully manages people or things on behalf of someone else or an organization. Even the things we believe we own outright do not belong to us forever. Life is never permanent but is given to us for a specific time and purpose. As 1 Timothy 6:7 reminds us, "For we brought nothing into this world, and it is certain we can carry nothing out."

Have you ever taken the time to inventory all your possessions and determine your most valuable asset? You might be surprised to learn that it's not your real estate, investments, boat, plane, jewelry, or expensive wardrobe, even if they are worth millions. When your time on Earth is up, none of these possessions will matter anymore. They can't help you or go with you. Someone else will enjoy your toys.

"For what shall it profit a man, if he shall gain the whole world, and lose his own soul?" (Mark 8:36)

This question is directed at anyone who is too focused on material things, too busy serving themselves, denying Christ, and pursuing the cares of the world. If you focus on saving your life, you will lose it. But if you lose your life now for the gospel's sake, you will save it for eternity. So, what is the benefit of focusing on gaining things you can never own eternally but only manage while here on Earth? What is the benefit of losing your soul for eternity? Your soul is the most valuable asset you will ever have stewardship over. You can replace real estate, investments, boats, planes, jewelry, and wardrobes. If you received them once, you can get them again. But your soul, your life, cannot be replaced. We only have one life, so handle it carefully and be the best steward of the most valuable thing you will ever possess.

God has blessed us with resources, but it's up to us to choose how we manage what He has given us. As Jesus said in the parable of the talents, "For unto whomsoever much is given, of him shall be much required" (Luke 12:48). If you're like me, you were not raised with money. I grew up on welfare in the '60s and '70s.

By today's standards, my mother was handicapped. She could not read or write, and she had a physical disability. But my mother was a praying woman who had faith in God and had a belt ministry. She'd whip you right where you acted up, whether in the grocery store or at home. And if she said shut up, you better do it quickly. Momma didn't play with children. She had a saying, "If you play with a dog, he'll lick your mouth. Play with a child; they will sass you out." Momma was a great steward over her children and the few things she had in life. She managed her four children as best as she could. Then, it was up to us to listen and apply what she taught us.

The University of Perseverance

Momma didn't have any degrees from the school system, but she had a Ph.D. from the University of Perseverance. She got her higher education from the University of Knee-ology, where she learned how to save and stretch her food until the end of the month. Momma often would fast while we ate because there was not enough food, but she made sure her four children were fed. She taught us to pray and have faith in God.

FICO scores were not being used back then. They were not used until 1989. As a mortgage loan officer, I would estimate that my mother's scores would have been in the high 700s to low 800s based on her discipline in paying her bills on time and not using debt as cash. There was a layaway system, and Momma always paid her layaway off on time.

My mother had even better credit with God. We lived in an older house at 261 S. 13th Street in Richmond, CA. It had two bedrooms and one bathroom. Momma was a woman of faith who spoke her desires into existence. In 1972, my mother prayed, "God, I want a brand-new home." She was the only person I knew with no job and no income but had mountain-moving faith and was an excellent steward. Her prayer was specific: "Brand new, four bedrooms, two bathrooms, $100.00 down payment." She prayed, put in the application, borrowed the money from her sister, and trusted God. A few months later, we moved into our new home as a family.

I've learned more about faith and stewardship from my mother than from anyone I've ever met or read about. She was a person with no formal education, business, or management experience. Yet, she valued prayer and faith in God, paid her debts on time and in full when possible, and avoided taking on too much debt. Above all, she cherished her name and reputation. They call this common sense, which, unfortunately, is not very common these days. Nowadays, people have formal education, business, and management experience, but are broke, have bad credit, and will not pay their bills on time because of misplaced priorities. We must change this and refocus on becoming debt-free and living beneath our means.

In 1984, when I became addicted to crack cocaine, my mother was going to church every Wednesday night, Friday night, Sunday morning, and Sunday night. Every time they had a prayer line, she would stand in line and request prayer, asking the church to keep praying for her drug-addicted son, that God would save and deliver him from crack cocaine. This she did for eight years. She was consistent, persistent, committed, and faithful in believing for her son's freedom from drugs. She maximized her effort, was a great steward of what God had given her, and she wanted me free from the demon of addiction.

I think of the story of the persistent widow in Luke 18:1-8, who kept coming to the unjust judge, pleading for justice against her adversary. Although the judge had no fear of God or regard for man, he finally granted her request because of her persistence. I also think of the parable of the lost coin in Luke 15:8-10, where the woman searched diligently until she found the one coin that was lost. Like these women, my mother persisted in prayer and faith until she saw her son saved, sanctified, and filled with the Holy Ghost. I have never met anyone like my mom. She truly maximized her heavenly FICO SCORES by always spending time with God.

I want to maximize my FICO SCORES with God as my mother did by spending quality time with Him and managing to perfection the things He has entrusted to me. I want to be a good steward over the lust in my eyes, the lust in my flesh, and the pride in my life. I want to be a good steward in my relationship with my wife, to be a better example to our grown children, and to be a great mentor to our grandchildren, especially in the areas where I fell short with my children. I want to encourage, edify, and correct when I see them going astray and celebrate them when they do well. I want to be a better leader to the members of the ministry that I pastor, not just a "Do as I say" leader, but a "Do as I do" leader, leading by example. I want to be a better co-worker and steward of the money God has entrusted me. I want to owe no man anything but love (Romans 13:8). I want to get out of debt and become debt-free to do more for the kingdom of God and my family. Let's all strive to be better stewards of everything God has placed under our care.

I have never met anyone like my mom.

The Parable of the Talents

In Matthew 25:14-30, Jesus tells the parable of the talents, comparing the kingdom of Heaven to a man traveling to a far country. Before leaving on his journey, the man called his servants and entrusted his possessions to them. To one servant, he gave five talents, to another two talents, and to another one talent, each according to his ability. Then he went on his journey.

The servant who received five talents immediately traded with them, gaining five more. Likewise, the servant with two talents gained two more. But the servant who received one talent buried it in the ground, hiding his lord's money. After a long time, the lord returned and settled accounts with his servants.

The servant who received five talents came forward and presented the additional five talents he gained, saying, "Lord, you delivered to me five talents; look, I have gained five more talents besides them." His lord commended him, saying, "Well done, good and faithful servant; you were faithful over a few things; I will make you ruler over many things. Enter into the joy of the lord."

The servant with two talents also came forward, presenting the two additional talents he had gained. He received the same commendation from his lord: "Well done, good and faithful servant. You were faithful over a few things; I will make you ruler over many things. Enter into the joy of the lord."

Then the servant who received one talent came forward and started by making excuses for his lack of productivity: "Lord, I knew you to be a hard man, reaping where you have not sown and gathering where you have not scattered seed. I was afraid of losing what you gave me, so I buried it in the ground." Instead of admitting his fear and procrastination upfront, he returned the talent, saying, "Here you go; you can have your talent back. I didn't do anything with it; I was too preoccupied with my own pursuits, unconcerned with your plans for my life, and doubted my ability to succeed." He concluded, "See, it's here safe and sound. I didn't lose it." Many people, like this man. They prioritize loss avoidance over pursuing the win.

This servant makes us think about how we handle what we've been given. Are we using our gifts, talents, and resources to their fullest, or are we holding back because we're scared or just comfortable where we are? Just as the servants who multiplied their talents, we also are called to be wise and brave with what we've got. We don't all start out with the same thing, but we are all given something according to our ability.

When we are faithful in small things, God can trust us with bigger responsibilities. It's not about how much you start with—it's about being faithful where we are with what we have, in order to be entrusted with more.

So, his lord rebuked him, calling him a wicked and lazy servant. He pointed out that, at the very least, the servant could have deposited the money with the bankers to earn interest. He commanded that the talent be taken from this servant and given to the one who has ten talents, saying, "For to everyone who has, more will be given, and he will have abundance; but from him who does not have, even what he has will be taken away."

I've wrestled with this story for years. How did the traveling man know which servant to give which talents to? I don't believe this was random. I can't say for sure, but I'm certain it wasn't based on looks, stature, age, or weight. I believe it was driven by relationships and past performance. Perhaps he had previously taken a trip and trusted these stewards. This was, in fact, the last time he would be testing the lazy steward.

The passage begins by comparing the kingdom of Heaven to the man preparing to travel. If the story is comparing the kingdom of Heaven—and God is a God of multiple chances—this was not the first time the man was tested. Just ask the children of Israel before they were taken into Babylonian captivity. They were warned for over 20 years by the prophet Jeremiah.

I believe the servant was given multiple opportunities. This time, the test was with talents, which represent gold in this passage. One talent of gold weighed about 75 pounds, which in today's market equals $2,358,000.00, a sum some people might value above all else. There is a saying: "Blood is thicker than water," with blood representing family and water representing friendships. Working in the financial industry since the early '90s, I've seen things that made me say, "Yeah, but green$$ is thicker than blood." God wants to know if He can trust you with money. Are you a good steward of what He has given you?

Based on past performance, I believe the traveler based his decision solely on competence. He left the first steward with five talents, the second with two talents, and the last, possibly on a Performance Improvement Plan (PIP), with one talent.

Immediately, the one who received the five talents—375 pounds of gold valued at $11,790,000.00—went and traded them, doubling the talents. The one with two talents—150 lbs. valued at $4,716,000.00—did the same. But the one on the PIP who received one talent buried it in the earth for fear of losing his lord's money. When we operate in fear, nothing gets done. In fact, we impede the progress of others. What we don't use wisely is taken and given to someone else because it's wasted in our hand.

This parable teaches us several important lessons about stewardship. First, God entrusts us with resources according to our ability to manage them. We are not all given the same amount, but we are all expected to be faithful with what we have been given.

Second, God expects us to use what He has given us to further His kingdom. The servants who invested their talents and gained more were commended as good and faithful servants. But the servant who buried his talent was rebuked for his wickedness and laziness.

Third, fear is not an excuse for failing to be a good steward. The servant buried his talent because he was afraid of losing it. But fear does not absolve us of our responsibility to use what God has given us for His glory.

Finally, there are rewards for faithfulness and consequences for unfaithfulness. The faithful servants were entrusted with greater responsibilities and invited to share in their master's joy. The unfaithful servant had even the little he had taken away from him.

As stewards of God's resources, we must remember that everything we have belongs to Him. We are simply managers entrusted with His possessions for a time.

> *"But who am I, and who are my people, that we should be able to offer so willingly as this? For all things come from You, and of Your own we have given You." (1 Chronicles 29:14)*

Our goal should be to hear our Master say, "Well done, good and faithful servant." This requires diligence, wisdom, and faithfulness in managing what He has given us. Whether entrusted with much or with little, we can be good stewards by using our resources to advance His kingdom, bless others, and bring glory to His name.

Remember, your most valuable asset is your soul. Take care of it, nurture it, and invest in your relationship with God. Be a good steward of the time, talents, and treasures He has entrusted you. As you do, you will see your heavenly FICO SCORES increase, and you will experience the joy and abundance that comes from living as a faithful steward of the King.

Cultivating a Heart of Gratitude

Being a good steward isn't just about managing resources; it's also about cultivating the right heart posture toward God, the ultimate owner of all things. One of the most powerful attitudes we can nurture is a heart of gratitude. Gratitude shifts our focus from what we lack to the abundance we already have in Christ. It aligns our hearts with the heart of God and positions us to receive even more of His blessings and favor.

Gratitude enables us to be better stewards of God's gifts. This profound truth can revolutionize your life and catapult your spiritual journey to unprecedented heights. Gratitude is the master key that unlocks the door to a life of abundance, joy, divine favor, and increased heavenly FICO SCORES.

We are commanded: "In every thing give thanks: for this is the will of God in Christ Jesus concerning you" (1 Thessalonians 5:18). Some might think, "How can I be thankful amid my pain, struggles, and trials?" Let me tell you, that's precisely when you need to practice gratitude the most.

Gratitude is not about denying your problems or pretending everything is perfect. No, it's about choosing to focus on the goodness of God, even when your circumstances are far from good. It's about remembering that God is still on the throne, that He is still in control, and that He is working all things together for your good, even when you can't see it.

When you cultivate a heart of gratitude, you make a conscious decision to shift your attention from your problems to your blessings. You magnify God's goodness rather than your own struggles. And let me tell you, that simple shift in perspective can change everything, including your heavenly credit standing with God.

Productive Trials

I remember a time when I was facing some serious challenges. My ministry was under attack, my family was going through a difficult season, and I felt like I was carrying the weight of the world on my shoulders. But amid that darkness, God reminded me of the power of gratitude.

I began to thank Him for the trials, knowing they produced perseverance, character, and hope (Romans 5:3-4). I thanked Him for the people He had placed in my life, even the ones who were causing me pain because I knew that God was using them to refine me and make me more like Christ. I thanked Him for His faithfulness, love, and grace, which sustained me.

As I began to practice gratitude, something miraculous happened in my heart. The heaviness started to lift, the joy began to return, and the peace that surpasses all understanding began to guard my heart and mind in Christ Jesus (Philippians 4:7). I realized that gratitude is not just a nice sentiment; it's a powerful spiritual weapon that can break the chains of despair, defeat, and discouragement. Moreover, as I expressed my gratitude to God, I could feel my heavenly FICO SCORES increasing, opening the door for more of His favor and blessings in my life.

But gratitude isn't just about getting through the hard times; it's also about living a life of abundance and blessing. When we cultivate a heart of gratitude, we position ourselves to receive the fullness of God's favor and provision. We align ourselves with His will and purposes and open the door for Him to pour His blessings into our lives. As our heavenly FICO SCORES increase through gratitude, we become more attuned to God's voice and more receptive to His guidance.

Soaring Examples

The Bible is full of examples of people who experienced the power of gratitude and saw their heavenly FICO SCORES soar. Take Mary, the mother of Jesus, for example. When the angel appeared to her and told her that she would give birth to the Son of God, she could have focused on the challenges and difficulties ahead. But instead, she chose to express her gratitude and praise to God. She declared, "My soul doth magnify the Lord, and my spirit hath rejoiced in God my Saviour" (Luke 1:46-47). As a result of her gratitude, Mary found favor with God and was blessed among women.

Or consider Paul and Silas, who were imprisoned for preaching the gospel. Instead of complaining about their circumstances, they chose to sing praises to God and give thanks for His goodness. And what happened? God sent an earthquake that shook the prison's foundations, broke their chains, and set them free (Acts 16:25-26). Their gratitude in the face of adversity not only increased their heavenly FICO SCORES but also opened the door for a miraculous deliverance.

The same power available to Mary, Paul, and Silas is available to you today. When you cultivate a heart of gratitude, you tap into a supernatural source of strength, joy, and victory. You declare to the enemy that he has no power over you because your hope and confidence are in the Lord. As you thank God, your heavenly FICO SCORES will continue to rise, bringing you closer to Him and positioning you for even more incredible blessings.

So, how do you cultivate a heart of gratitude? It starts with a decision to make thankfulness a daily practice. Begin each day by thanking God for His goodness and mercy. Thank Him for the breath in your lungs, the roof over your head, and the food on your table. Thank Him for the people He has placed in your life, even the ones who challenge you because they are helping you grow and mature in Christ.

Gratitude Journal

Keep a gratitude journal and write down three to five things you're thankful for each day. Share your testimonies of God's goodness with others and encourage them to do the same. Make gratitude a central part of your prayer life, thanking God for His answers and provision before you even see them manifest in your life.

When the trials and challenges come, as they inevitably will, choose to give thanks in the midst of them. Remember that God is with you, He is for you, and He is working all things together for your good. Declare His promises over your life, and trust that He will bring you through to the other side. As you maintain an attitude of gratitude, even in tough times, your heavenly FICO SCORES will continue to climb, drawing you closer to God and His abundant blessings.

As you cultivate a heart of gratitude, you will begin to see your life transformed from the inside out. You will experience a new level of joy, peace, and contentment from knowing that God is in control and working all things together for His glory and your good. You will become a magnet for His blessings and favor and see Him open doors no man can shut. Your heavenly FICO SCORES will soar, reflecting the depth of your relationship with God and your trust in His goodness.

So today, choose to embrace gratitude as a way of life. Choose to focus on God's goodness, even amid your challenges. Give thanks in all circumstances, knowing this is God's will for you in Christ Jesus. Watch as He transforms your heart, mind, and life through gratitude, elevating your heavenly FICO SCORES to new heights.

Remember, a grateful heart is a receptive heart. When you give thanks, you open yourself to receive all God has for you. You position yourself for breakthrough, favor, and abundance. You become a living testimony of His goodness and grace and shine His light in a dark and hurting world.

Ultimately, being a good steward is about managing everything in our lives with an attitude of gratitude. When we approach our time, talents, resources, and relationships with a heart of thankfulness, we honor God as the Giver of all good things. We acknowledge that everything we have is a gift from Him, entrusted to us for a season. As we faithfully steward what He has given with gratitude, He can trust us with even more responsibilities and blessings. Let us commit to being good and faithful stewards, magnifying the Lord in every area of our lives and giving thanks always for His abundant provision.

May the Lord bless you and keep you as you cultivate a heart of gratitude. May He make His face shine upon you and be gracious to you. May He lift His countenance upon you and give you peace. May you experience the fullness of His joy, provision, and favor as you walk in thankfulness all the days of your life, watching your heavenly FICO SCORES rise to unprecedented levels. In Jesus' name, amen.

Epilogue

As we conclude this transformative journey, I trust and pray you have gained a deeper understanding of the incredible potential within you to live a life of purpose, fulfillment, and intimacy with God. Together, we have explored fundamental principles and strategies to unlock the abundant blessings and favor God has in store for each of us.

Throughout this book, we have emphasized the importance of cultivating unwavering faith, embracing our true identity in Christ, walking in obedience and righteousness, and stewarding the gifts and resources entrusted to us. We have also discussed the power of commitment, the process of sanctification, and the daily choice to prioritize seeking the kingdom of God and His righteousness.

As you prepare to close these pages, remember this is not the end but just the beginning of your journey. The truths and insights you have discovered are not merely intellectual concepts but practical tools for daily application. To aid in this ongoing journey of growth and transformation, I again encourage you to engage with the *10 Keys to Maximizing Your Heavenly FICO SCORES Workbook*. It is designed to help you internalize and implement the principles discussed, offering practical exercises, thought-provoking questions, and opportunities for personal reflection.

Always remember, you are never alone on this journey. God is with you every step of the way, guiding, strengthening, and empowering you to live out the purpose and potential He has placed within you. He who began this good work in you is faithful to complete it (Philippians 1:6).

So, continue pressing forward with perseverance. Seek God's face earnestly, choosing obedience over compromise, faith over fear, and righteousness over fleeting pleasures. In doing so, you will grow in wisdom, maturity, and intimacy with God, experiencing the joy and peace that comes from aligning your life with His will and walking in the abundance of His blessings.

Your spiritual growth will naturally elevate your life to new heights, not through striving or earning, but through a life fully devoted to God. As you live out these truths, you will become a beacon of His goodness and grace, shining brightly in a world in need of hope and love found only in Christ.

As you embark on the next phase of your journey, armed with the insights and tools from this book, dream big, pray boldly, and trust wholeheartedly in the God who exceeds all expectations (Ephesians 3:20). Embrace the adventure of faith, knowing that the best is yet to come and that God has extraordinary plans for your future.

May you continue to grow in your heavenly journey, not just for personal gain but for the glory of God and the advancement of His kingdom. May you be a catalyst for change, a bearer of hope, and a reflection of Christ's love to everyone you encounter. May every area of your life overflow with God's favor, blessing, and purpose.

Thank you for joining me on this journey to unlock the abundant life God intends for each of us. It has been an honor and privilege to share these truths with you. I eagerly anticipate seeing how God will continue to work in and through you as you put these principles into practice.

Remember, your story is still being written, with the best chapters yet to come. Keep writing, growing, and pursuing the incredible destiny

God has prepared uniquely for you. May His grace, peace, and abundance accompany you always, as your journey continues to elevate your heavenly FICO SCORES through obedience and faith.

With anticipation for all that God will accomplish in you, through you, for and with you!

—Pastor Don

10 Keys to Maximizing Your Heavenly FICO SCORES Workbook

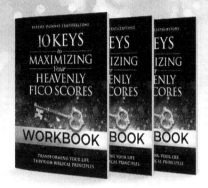

This transformative workbook will guide you on a journey of self-discovery and spiritual growth through practical exercises, biblical insights, thought-provoking questions, and powerful prayers. Whether you're a new believer or a seasoned Christian, this workbook is designed to meet you where you are and help you take your faith to new heights.

- Cultivate unwavering faith and embrace your God-given identity
- Walk in obedience and integrity
- Develop a heart of gratitude and stewardship
- Unlock God's favor and blessing in your life

Don't settle for a mediocre spiritual life. Invest in your relationship with God and watch as your heavenly FICO SCORES soar.

ISBN 9781562296469 | 8.5"x11" | Paperback | 34 pages

Available wherever books are sold and from ChristianLivingBooks.com.

Dedication

To My Lovely Wife: A Tribute of Endless Love and Support

Wifelit, your unwavering support, boundless love, and endless encouragement have been my guiding light throughout our 31 years of marriage. You believed in me and took a chance, marrying me after only one year of being delivered from an eight-year crack addiction, with no job and living with my mom. You saw the potential in me and brought out the best in me when everyone else only saw what I used to be. You accepted my hand in marriage and took me in, and for that, I am eternally grateful.

"A man's greatest treasure is his wife—she is a gift from the Lord."
(Proverbs 18:22 CEV)

Thank you for believing in me and encouraging me to accept the bank teller job, which launched my career into FICO scores, even though I felt it was beneath me. Despite everything we've gone through—the ups and downs, the highs and lows, the good and the bad, the sunshine and the rain, from the bitter to the sweet, whether happy or sad, through agreeing and disagreeing—our love has endured.

Your faithfulness is a beacon in my life. Grounded and centered in your faith, you put God first in everything you do. Your dedication to fasting and praying not only strengthens your relationship with God but also fortifies ours. You embody the spirit of unwavering faith, and your commitment to living a life centered around Christ is truly inspiring. Our love is enduring and eternal, like the scripture in Psalms 1:3 CEV: "They are like trees growing beside a stream, trees that produce fruit in season and always have leaves. Those people succeed in everything they do." (That's us.)

My love for you is unmovable and unstoppable until death do us part. An endless love! This book is a testament to the strength and inspiration you provide every day. With all my love, Hublet!

To My Church Family: A Celebration of Faith, Unity, and Service

With immense gratitude and humility, I also dedicate this book to the faithful members, both past and present, of Faith Temple Empowerment Church—a ministry committed to fostering deliberate deliverance. Together, we pray, praise, worship, and study the Word of God, growing in unity and believing that everything is possible through Christ. I am eternally grateful to God for entrusting me with the responsibility of leading His people in this anointed ministry of deliverance, where people can come and receive what they need spiritually, akin to a trauma center. Though our numbers may be small, our strength lies in our unwavering faith, making us a mighty force—a courageous army of the Lord. Serving you faithfully is an honor I will always cherish. You are indeed a chosen generation, a royal priesthood, the holy people of God, the peculiar ones who praise our Savior through words and actions. This moment fills me with profound joy.

FTEC, you are well acquainted with my heart and the transparency with which I have shared my experiences of life's highs and lows. While I do not claim to have all the answers concerning the Bible or life, I possess the knowledge to guide us toward healing, deliverance from sin, freedom from financial burdens, and, ultimately, the path to Heaven. As a pastor, it grieves me deeply to witness individuals losing faith in themselves and God when confronted with life's trials.

Reflecting on our journey together, I am inspired by how our church has focused on pleasing God, helping each other, and living out our faith through acts of love, care, and support. We've been motivated to share Christ by letting our light shine, even when our voices are silent. Our collective commitment to studying the Word of God strengthens our community and amplifies our witness to the world. As we discern God's voice and distinguish it from our own and the enemy's, we grow in our understanding of His divine plan and find the abundant life promised by Christ. Your collective inspiration has driven me to write this book for anyone who desires to strengthen their faith in God and themselves by embracing His divine plan for their lives.

About the Author

Pastor Donnie R. Featherstone did not accept Christ at an early age. After becoming disillusioned with a dead-end lifestyle, he came to Jesus on December 18, 1990, and was filled with the precious gift of the Holy Ghost. Unfortunately, he backslid a couple of months later, succumbing to the call of crack cocaine. God reclaimed him, and he finally submitted to His will on January 17, 1992. He came to Jesus just as he was: "tore up from the floor up—beat down from the feet down." God delivered him from an eight-year crack addiction.

Unemployed and armed with a high school diploma and a few community college credits, Pastor Don began seeking the kingdom of God. God quickly elevated his heavenly FICO SCORES, blessing him both spiritually and naturally.

Pastor Don has been married to Leading Lady Shirley Featherstone for over 30 years. They have a beautiful family comprising seven children, 15 grandchildren, and one great-grandson.

In July 1998, Pastor Don was ordained as an Elder in the Church of God in Christ (COGIC) under the late Bishop Jessie W. Dickens of the California Western Ecclesiastical Jurisdiction. In February

2002, he was installed as the Senior Pastor of Faith Temple Empowerment Church (FTEC) in Richmond, California. Pastor Don has served in numerous capacities on the jurisdictional level, including Evangelist President, Chief Adjutant, District Superintendent, and Administrative Assistant. Nationally, he serves as a National Adjutant for COGIC, Inc., and currently serves under Bishop Bob Jackson in the California West Coast Jurisdiction as a Pastor and Jurisdictional Chief Adjutant.

As Senior Pastor of FTEC, a powerful church of deliverance, the vision is to build bridges to the kingdom of God by equipping individuals and families, empowering them in the Word, family, life, health, and work. The mission is PEOPLE: Persons Exhorting Others to Promote Learning and Ethics. Pastor Don has dedicated the past quarter-century to working with the broken, forgotten, and less fortunate to rebuild hope in God and self-worth. Through faithful teaching and preaching of deliverance, many lives have been transformed from drugs, alcohol, and the scars of abuse. God is faithfully delivering people from the power of darkness.

Pastor Don's concern and compassion for the hurting, lost, broken, destitute, and homeless are evident in his ministry. He ministers to youth not only within the church building but also on street corners, at the mall, and in other public places, mentoring them regardless of race or ethnicity. He encourages them to develop a thirst for truth and learning through reading, studying, and trusting the process of life. He urges them to believe in God and in themselves, no matter where they were born because the world is waiting for them.

He advises them not to let distractions from what they see others doing prevent them from discovering their true identity through God. There is a place for them, and the answers they seek lie within. New opportunities await beyond their current circumstances and are ready to be discovered by those with the determination to seek and the courage to pursue them. "You can do all things through Christ who strengthens you" (Philippians 4:13).

His dedication to working and struggling families, barely getting by, and supporting parents is deeply touching. Pastor Don strives to be a beacon of hope, offering guidance and support to those in need. His care for these individuals is rooted in his own experiences, understanding the struggles they face. He often reminds others that their story is not broken; God can use it to help others avoid similar pitfalls.

Pastor Don's ministry extends beyond preaching and teaching. He engages with the community through food drives, clothing donations, and outreach programs to ensure that those often overlooked receive the care and attention they deserve. However, he emphasizes that, like Jesus, who fed the thousands only twice, his ministry's primary focus is on healing, bringing deliverance, and restoring sight to the spiritually blind and the spiritually lame.

Pastor Don is bio-vocational, employed by JP Morgan Chase for over 13 years as a Senior Mortgage Lender in Berkeley, California, with 26 years in the lending industry. He is a former Chaplain for the San Francisco Sheriff Department Peer Support and a First Responder (2004-2013). He has held various professional licenses as a California Real Estate Agent and State Notary. Pastor Don received an undergraduate degree in Biblical Studies from Sacramento Seminary, an autodidactic Graduate Degree from the School of Hard Knocks, and an honorary doctorate from the University of Adversity.

In life, pain is temporary, but God's glory is forever!

Made in the USA
Columbia, SC
31 October 2024

45295262R00087